T0307888

ADVANCE PRAISE FOR
A QUIET FOGHORN

"A must-read book that gives a poignant, sometimes funny, and always fascinating insight into the life of a Deaf gay man. With a clear voice, Raymond Luczak provides a deeply personal account of the joys, sorrows, and insights that come from his fascinating life experience."

—Lennard J. Davis, author of
My Sense of Silence: Memoirs of a Childhood with Deafness

"This exuberant, highly readable collection opens Luczak's world— both his personal world and his broader worlds as a Deaf gay man, a writer, a creative, and a member of interlinked communities— and invites us to share in celebrating the beauty of his life. These essays speak to me of radical joy, which is a rare, transcendent, and sustaining quality that we as readers need now."

—Kelly Davio, author of
It's Just Nerves: Notes on a Disability

"With *A Quiet Foghorn*, Raymond Luczak again provides us with the life-sustaining exploration of Deaf and queer life that has characterized all his work. This is a book about the importance of connecting with others, pushing through loneliness and fear to the joy that comes from discovering and sustaining community."

—Robert McRuer, author of
Crip Theory: Cultural Signs of Queerness and Disability

A QUIET FOGHORN

A QUIET FOGHORN

more notes from a deaf gay life

RAYMOND LUCZAK

GALLAUDET UNIVERSITY PRESS
Washington, DC

Gallaudet University Press
gupress.gallaudet.edu

Gallaudet University Press is located on the traditional territories of Nacotchtank
and Piscataway.

© 2022 by Raymond Luczak
All rights reserved. Published 2022
Printed in the United States of America

ISBN 978-1-954622-11-1 (paperback)
ISBN 978-1-954622-12-8 (ebook)

Library of Congress Cataloging-in-Publication Data

Names: Luczak, Raymond, 1965- author.
Title: A quiet foghorn : more notes from a deaf gay life / Raymond Luczak.
Description: Washington, DC : Gallaudet University Press, 2022. | Summary:
   "This is an essay collection by deaf writer Raymond Luczak"-- Provided
   by publisher.
Identifiers: LCCN 2022012571 (print) | LCCN 2022012572 (ebook) | ISBN
   9781954622111 (paperback ; alk. paper) | ISBN 9781954622128 (ebook)
Subjects: LCGFT: Essays.
Classification: LCC PS3562.U2554 Q54 2022 (print) | LCC PS3562.U2554
   (ebook) | DDC 814/.54--dc23/eng/20220622
LC record available at https://lccn.loc.gov/2022012571
LC ebook record available at https://lccn.loc.gov/2022012572

∞ This paper meets the requirements of ANSI/NISO Z39.48–1992 (Permanence
of Paper).

Cover description: Against a vignette-style blue background, a photo of a foghorn
from below. It is centered and angled so that the slightly arched title text at the top
of the cover resembles sound waves emerging from the horn. The title reads, A Quiet
Foghorn, with the letters in the words a quiet in different pastel colors: yellow, green,
blue, purple, orange, and red; the word foghorn in white. Smaller black text is the
subtitle: more notes from a deaf gay life. At the bottom is the author's name in white:
Raymond Luczak.

Cover design by Mona Z. Kraculdy
Cover photograph by Adam Kauwenberg-Marsnik

While the author has made every effort to provide accurate internet addresses and
other contact information at the time of publication, neither the publisher nor the
author assumes any responsibility for errors or changes that occur after publication.
Further, the publisher does not have any control over and does not assume any
responsibility for third-party websites or their content.

in memory of my Deaf elders

Jack Randle Gannon
1936–2022

Nathie Lee Marbury
1944–2013

Mary Beth Miller
1942–2019

Nellie Jane Norman
1939–2020

Guy Charles Wonder Jr.
1945–2020

CONTENTS

A NOTE TO THE READER

This book is a collection of essays written over the last twenty years. It is only natural that time would affect the shifts and changes in the tempo of such writing as my views as a Deaf gay man evolved from then to now.

The capitalized "D" in the word "deaf" is used to indicate a cultural and linguistic—as in American Sign Language (ASL)—perspective on deafness, as opposed to the medical and educational establishment's view of deafness as a medical condition that must be corrected.

OF BLOOD, BORN

A QUIET FOGHORN

Everyone knew I was different the second I opened my mouth and made a sound. The second before I had looked like them: I had a perfectly formed mouth and a set of good teeth.

I speak through my nose. There's a reason for that. Many deaf children, when they learn how to speak, cannot sense the physical relationship between lungs inside the ribcage and the weird sounds that they are asked to produce. Speech therapists go for the next best thing, which is to focus on the throat where sounds can be easily felt. They get more discernible results that way.

For years, I used to hate the sound of my voice.

I didn't want to see how hearing people's eyes flickered ever so slightly the second they heard me speak.

I didn't want to see how they tried not to look more closely at the earmolds inside my ears.

I didn't want to see how they tried to hide their discomfort with my make-do speech.

I have been seen as a freak for so long that I've become numb to such subtle shifts in behavior.

But is being numb a good thing?

Perhaps it's a good survival mechanism while young and lost in a world that didn't always make sense from a child's perspective.

The older I get, the less patient I am with pretending to be "nice." I am tired of feeling numb. I speak up more and demand eye contact. I find myself feeling more emotions far more quickly than I ever did as a child.

———

Being deaf, I cannot fully hear myself. I do not know what I truly sound like, or whether all the intended sounds in my speech are fully formed. Many of my consonants are missing. But I have always wanted to be a singer, more so when MTV flourished during the Golden Age of Music Videos circa the first half of the 1980s. The singers around whom cameras revolved had all the attention. Nearly naked women fawned over skinny men with permed mullets as they lip-synched to their latest hit. Occasionally, a coterie of tuxedoed men would center around a female singer, like Madonna in the "Material Girl" video, where she infamously paid tribute to Marilyn Monroe, but that was rare.

As a budding deaf homosexual, I sensed that it was taboo to have a group of men interested in a woman, but it was totally natural to have a group of near-naked women prancing about in front of the cameras. I never questioned the nature of these things; I was too afraid to ask why there weren't more men in the music videos.

I watched for the men anyway.

In the video for Olivia Newton-John's massive hit "Physical," she coyly walked through an all-male gym. Here and there, I caught a sly glance of desire between men while she shrugged it off with a boys-will-always-be-boys look. I had to wonder whether it was indeed possible for bodybuilders to be physically interested in each other.

Some textbooks say that adolescence is a time of constant questioning. I questioned the changes in my body every day in front of the bathroom mirror. Here I was, all of 5'11" and 126 pounds. My pectorals were flat, and I didn't have much of an ass. The sensation of peach fuzz soon turning to darker and stiffer hairs on my jaw did not lose its strangeness for the longest time. The sprouting of chest hair and the sharp tang of my underarms didn't help matters.

But worse were the pimples that dotted like weeds all over my freckled face. I came to hate them because no matter how gingerly I coaxed out the sebum, it left behind a hint of blood that took a day or two to heal. By then, other pimples popped up elsewhere. I envied my hearing classmates who didn't seem to have acne, and those who did seemed to have minor zits that soon vanished.

I observed them all each day in the classroom. I hungered to touch the muscles of these young men bursting with braggadocio, but I knew it was hopeless. If I was too afraid to touch myself in the same way I ached to touch another man's body, how could I possibly hope to touch another?

There is a certain power to be gleaned from stillness. I had to sit still in the classroom and not move while lipreading for hours. I had to work to understand. I sometimes resented how hearing classmates could doodle on their notebook margins without once looking up at the teacher.

Why not me? Why couldn't I look cool with my wireless hearing aid? In those days my hearing teachers wore a bulky microphone around their necks to enable me to hear their voices more clearly. Looking cool was impossible.

And yet, thanks to my hands, I've learned the greater power of silence. Hearing people who don't know how to sign are forced to look more closely at me, trying to glean meanings from my hands. Their eyes dart all over the place.

Out in the woods, across the street from the house where I grew up, I made percussive sounds with the clicking of my tongue and the sharp hums of my throat. Sometimes I tried singing in a nasal falsetto, which I'm sure sounded awful to any hearing person, but to me, I felt a private joy in deluding myself that I was indeed a pop singer in the making.

The pop star thing never happened. I became a quiet foghorn instead.

MY TRUEST HOME

I remember Mom waking me gently, and then firmly, at five in the morning, to bundle up for our annual trip from Ironwood to Marquette, where I'd undergo an audiological exam at Northern Michigan University to determine whether my hearing over the past year had changed or not. The trip usually took three hours under good weather conditions, but it was January, and that meant we had to think about the patches of ice on the highway.

Once sealed inside the soundproof room and observed through layers of murky gray-tinted windows by the audiologist, I raised my hand whenever I thought I'd detected the faintest murmur of sound in my headphones. I also repeated what I could comprehend: *Say the word "airplane." Say the word "cowboy." Say the word "hot dog."*

The whole trip was bearable because I could be alone with Mom for a long period of time without interruption from my eight siblings. The closeness I'd felt toward her was most apparent on those occasions whenever I sensed she wanted to be away from everyone for a while. Our visits to Marquette were among her chances to be free for a day; she almost never had a break from us.

Because I was the only deaf student in Ironwood, my parents decided that it was best for me to attend a speech program for deaf students from all over the western Upper Peninsula in Houghton, a two-hour ride away. Starting at age four, I stayed with a foster family from Sunday nights to Friday afternoon, when a college student in Houghton would pick me up at school and drive me home to my biological family.

Even though I traveled back to Ironwood on Friday nights and to Houghton on Sunday nights, I never considered the road a part of me until those moments on our way to Marquette for my annual audiological exam when I saw how Mom enjoyed herself, talking with the driver and his other passengers in his station wagon. Did she really like the road? I simply saw it as a way back home, but shuttling between families for a total of nine years meant that the word "home" would acquire a nebulous meaning.

Mom has always maintained that no one would ever confirm how I'd lost so much of my hearing. As such, I've always dated my deafness from the last possible cause—a bout of double pneumonia—at the age of eight months. She has recounted many times how—in the middle of a notorious heat wave—she noticed how feverish I'd become, and how she and Dad had thought I'd die. The day was July 9, 1966: I think of it as the first, and probably the most crucial, turning point of my life.

My sister Carole noticed that something was amiss after I returned from the hospital. She liked to read out loud to me in the crib; I had always been keen to listen to what she'd say next. Now I didn't seem to respond to her voice at all. But it was not until I was two and a half years old when my parents finally conceded that something was indeed wrong. Before I knew it, a huge hearing aid was strapped to my tiny chest.

I recall nothing of that hearing aid, which had to be recharged every night. But I do remember Mom holding my hand as we walked toward Norrie Elementary School on a bright September afternoon. The skies were a spectacular blue, with just a few clouds moving north. Children filed out of the doors; school had been just dismissed. In an empty classroom on the second floor, my first speech therapist awaited me. Mom sat next to me, nodding and smiling whenever I got a sound right, or grasped the words beneath mimeographed pictures. I don't remember the speech therapist at all, but I do remember the word MAN beneath a businessman with a hat and a briefcase. I thought of it for a long time: perhaps it was because everywhere I went, I'd seen so few men—if at all—wearing three-piece suits. It was the very first speech therapy session that I could remember; I wasn't even three at the time.

Mom also accompanied me on Saturday afternoons to my

private First Communion classes with Sister Virgene at Ironwood Catholic Grade School. I loved writing inside this one book with a shiny gold lamé cover as Sister Virgene peered at me through her pointed glasses. I was full of hush.

St. Michael's Church on McLeod Street was *the* reference point of each weekend with my family in Ironwood, away from Houghton. When we went to Mass, it was only a matter of hours before I went back to Houghton. St. Michael's was the same church where all my grandparents attended, Mom and Dad were married in, and my siblings were given their First Communion. The thing I remember most from attending Masses was how we had to walk on the left side of the main aisle in order to sit somewhere in the middle rows of the left front quarter of pews: Father Frank's pulpit was on the left side, which was supposed to make it easier for me to speechread him. But he had a very soft voice; I never understood a word he'd said. I did follow along with a children's guidebook to Mass, which had lovely photographs of a priest conducting each ritual. When I think about it now, the shiny solemnity of these pictures had recaptured best for me what the Mass should've been about: a time for reflection on oneself. Instead, because I couldn't always speechread Father Frank (and other priests as well), I took to daydreaming about what I'd do the minute we got out of church.

Yet, during my childhood in Houghton, I never gave thought to whether speech therapy had made me different from the other kids on the playground; I played with my deaf classmates then. There were only five of us at any given time in the classroom. But the more mainstreamed I became, the more I came to understand that those things in my ears had made me different from my hearing classmates. My years at Ironwood Catholic emphasized that feeling of differentness inside me. It was as if I was no longer fully me, but I wasn't quite aware of how it could be so.

All that changed one summer when I saw my brother David *asking* for speech therapy with Mrs. Fraites. I couldn't comprehend the meaning of the word *lisp* until years later when I became more aware of various speech impediments after spending the summer of 1981 at Bay Cliff Health Camp. At the time, though, I was baffled;

while I loved Mrs. Fraites (it was hard not to), I couldn't imagine anyone *asking* to go through the repetition of sounds that caused so much difficulty and embarrassment. I watched from a distance as David and Mrs. Fraites sat at the rickety picnic table under the apple tree in our backyard. I'd thought speech therapy was always for people who wore hearing aids (I'd never quite thought of myself as deaf, for I wasn't yet exposed to the radical idea of assuming one's disability as part of one's identity), and I never knew—or more accurately, couldn't perceive—David's speech problem.

So what did I know about belonging in a hearing class? I stayed full-time in Ironwood Catholic School starting in fifth grade, when teachers in Houghton felt I'd do equally well, requiring only speech therapy with Mrs. Fraites. After two years, I became tired of not being accepted by my classmates. I was tired of being good and getting no tangible reward for it, not even a friend. So one afternoon in seventh grade, when we each got a huge advertisement explaining the costs and specifics of our school pictures, I decided to doodle moustaches, moles, and birthmarks all over the faces of kids on the flyer. My classmates roared at my sudden defiance and responded with attempts to outdo my outrageousness.

I was apprehended and sent to the principal's office. It was then I knew I couldn't win friends in my class, not if I remained good. These years found me feeling incredibly lonely, and I turned more and more to writing as my salvation.

Back then, speech seemed like a powerful drug. It was supposed to be my ticket into the usually inscrutable hearing world, and I thought if they made fun of my speech, they'd stop if they knew how much I appreciated their musical interests.

One afternoon, Mom walked through the living room while I played Nick Gilder's "Hot Child in the City." At the time, I didn't understand that it was about a young prostitute, or that it was about wanting to have sex with her. All I could grasp was the title's repetition, and it was not long before I was able to chant along with it, and in the right places too. She hated the record because it was "so dirty"; I felt an embarrassment of pink rising in my ears. I couldn't understand how something that sounded so memorable could be so bad, but it was not until the summer of 1982 that I finally understood the subliminal seduction of rock and roll.

That summer, my sister Vivien and I were looking around at albums and 45s in Johnson's Music Store, dreaming and hoping for the day we'd be able to afford to buy any record we wanted. I'd just heard the Beatles leap from one song snippet to another in their "Movie Medley," pieced together from original songs to promote *Reel Music*, a collection of their soundtrack hits. I loved the thunderous opening of "Magical Mystery Tour," and as *Magical Mystery Tour* was cheaper than *Reel Music*, I took that one. I didn't have much money, but the Beatles were one group I *had* to have that summer. While I waited in line, Father Frank—he'd then retired from St. Michael's—wandered into the store. He lost his smile when he saw the Beatles album in my hands. I didn't understand what I'd just done, but that was my first act of rebellion against the Church. We told no one about Father Frank's reaction, but we listened to the Beatles with a passion. With each record that I brought home, I expressed in my own way the unspoken desire to truly be myself.

Mom gave disapproving glances whenever I played a song that she knew was much more explicit than she'd care to give credit for. It was with some irony that she loved Boy George singing "Karma Chameleon." I was simply happy to know that she liked his voice, because I secretly wanted to be as outrageous as Boy George—not with my appearance, but through a who-cares-what-they-think attitude. I just didn't have the guts to be cool; I came to understand a few years later that cool came from *within*, on my own terms, and that my cool didn't have to be derived from the hearing world itself.

In "Passport," a chapter from my novel *Men with Their Hands*, Michael and Nick are twelve years old, and best friends; Michael is deaf, Nick is not. What happens next on their school playground is a painful rite of passage for many deaf people in hearing schools:

> Nick walks over to a group of boys standing around talking.
> Michael follows. He has to follow if he doesn't want to be

laughed at. He knows that Kerry, the tallest boy in the bunch, already smokes cigarettes, that Mikey has already fingered Jana, the most developed girl in their class: All this Nick has told him. In fact, almost everything he knows about his classmates has come from Nick; the boys talk too fast for Michael to lipread. Why couldn't they just play Nerf football, or tag? He doesn't like this change in their ways. They are no longer playing; they want to *talk* like all those grown-ups he knows . . .

He knows he is going to *hate* growing up. If the boys were always laughing, and if he can't always understand their jokes, he knows he will be miserable. The kids in his hearing-impaired classroom are always boring; they never want to try anything new or outrageous the way Nick always does. He likes Nick best when he dares to try something different: once, Nick stuffed two balloons into his pale green parka jacket and pulled a print apron tightly over his waist for the Halloween fest in the gym downstairs. Everyone broke out into peals of laughter, and it was one of the few times he'd really understood why they were laughing, and the only time he felt totally un-self-conscious about laughing along with them.

But something that's funny is killed when it has to be repeated so soon after its first occurrence. The joke is no longer spontaneous, it sounds contrived. It can work only if it's unintended in the moment of inspiration. Having to endure such secondhand humor is another reason Michael knows he will hate growing up.

That Michael couldn't follow the conversation at hand may be seen as a tragedy, but that he didn't have enough self-confidence to assert his need to understand—without an iota of shame—is a greater tragedy that persists today. Growing up, I too did not have the tools that would've empowered me to speak up and demand access. I had simply believed that my communication needs didn't matter all that much. Others were hearing, after all.

Speech therapy doesn't always show deaf people how to be proud of their speech when their speech isn't that clear except to those familiar with "deaf speech." And how can Michael speak the words to describe why he feels so ambivalent if it's already difficult for him to enunciate in the first place? Without an ounce of self-confidence—or even being allowed to communicate whatever is most comfortable for them—no Deaf[1] person could ever possibly learn to fend for themselves; that is perhaps the greatest tragedy in the educational history of Deaf people.

At fourteen, I suddenly spoke up. I told Mrs. Fraites, my speech therapist, that I needed to learn sign language. She was surprised, but she complied with my request. That was how Mary Hoffman entered my life, with a big binder of photocopied signs, which were based on Signing Exact English (SEE); I wouldn't learn until a few years later that SEE, although derived from many ASL signs, was really a system for teaching English to Deaf students. With each SEE sign that I picked up very rapidly, I sensed I had been given the very weapon for my own liberation. I felt ecstatic, signing alone to the woods across the street and in the dark before I fell asleep. I didn't realize it at the time, but my hands, once freed, began to tap into my unarticulated hatred of speech therapy.

I gradually became disillusioned because I realized I was *the* exception: parents want to believe their child is the exception. The problem was, I didn't want to be an exception. I wanted to be like everyone else, as I soon discovered upon my arrival as a freshman at Gallaudet University. I wasn't unique; everyone else was Deaf too!

When I adopted ASL at that time, I knew I had to answer this question—how many deaf people did I know who could claim to write and speak as well as I did?—before I could call myself *Deaf*.[1] Why had I succeeded when others didn't? I was eager to learn, yes, and I had enough residual hearing that enabled me to distinguish between many sounds. But I think that was because I was often away from Ironwood; I thought I had done something bad to be sent away, and thought I had to be so good that I'd never have to be sent back to Houghton. It soon became a habitual state of mind, and

---

1. The capitalized "D" in the word "deaf" is used to indicate a cultural and linguistic—as in American Sign Language (ASL)—perspective on deafness, as opposed to the medical and educational establishment's view of deafness as a medical condition that must be corrected.

it was not until I began asking myself why I accepted speech therapy so enthusiastically when I found myself hating it so much that I discovered the reason.

No doctor, audiologist, speech therapist, teacher, or surgeon should ever pretend to cure deafness, or make us over into people with "a hearing problem." When we grow up not hearing as well as others, our deafness does become a state of mind whether we want it to or not. Consequently, we value communication much more than most hearing people I know.

After graduating from Gallaudet, I worked as a substitute teacher at the Lexington School for the Deaf in Queens. On my last day, I went down to the auditorium to watch the children each draw a name of their classmates to whom they'd give a Christmas gift. Watching the teachers trying to communicate to these children without using ASL made me cringe, not because they didn't sign at all but because they were making exaggerated movements of their mouths (and their faces). I felt insulted by such blatant baby talk: Where was the respect of understanding due these intelligent children? When I left later that day, I felt so relieved because I knew if I'd stayed on as a teacher's assistant, I'd have blown up sooner or later.

If we are exasperated with how Deaf children are educated, many interpreters share it as well. One interpreter told me of the one time she'd fought so hard not to blow up at the speech therapist working with a Deaf student. She had been hired as a classroom interpreter; she usually sat in the room during the hours she didn't have to work. The student was sixteen years old, and his speech therapist was struggling with him to pronounce the sound "k." He couldn't produce it properly, and after an hour of trying not to feel pity for him—and anger at the speech therapist—the interpreter watched as the student was finally able to produce one perfect "k." The speech therapist exclaimed, "Now you can really learn to speak!" After the interpreter told me this, she added, "Why do they have to have speech therapy when he could've been learning so much more about the world itself? All that time wasted, and for what?"

When I was seventeen, I erupted at Mom and Dad. "You know something? I never really felt like I was a part of the family." It must've seemed that I'd thrown all their efforts to treat me like everyone else right out the window. I realize now that I had gone one step further than most deaf children with their hearing parents. Most of them would rather pretend that nothing was wrong whenever they visited, because it would be too awkward to communicate in the first place. Yes, I'd dared to verbalize the angst of being treated like everyone else when I knew I was *different*; it was among the many steps I had to take in order to become my own person, whether as a writer, or a deaf adolescent, or a gay man.

Of course, two years later, after my first semester at Gallaudet, Mom and Dad became more quiet and hurt when they learned I'd left the Catholic Church, had come out as a gay man, and had fallen for a DeafBlind technical assistant for a theater. It seemed as if the world they'd envisioned for me had gone awry: Every teacher and speech therapist had told them I'd go far with my capabilities. What had made them so delighted with me was not only my intelligence but also the true potential of my good speech; I could become a doctor, a lawyer, or a professor. Even Mrs. Fraites thought I could become an ear doctor and set up my practice in Ironwood; what she—or most hearing people—didn't grasp was that if I were to be successful, I needed not to deny my deafness but to reaffirm it as part of my identity.

In the four years of rewriting since its original conception, my first book of poems *St. Michael's Fall* was to be a diatribe against the Church. Nothing worked. What I needed to realize, after taking Marilyn Hacker's workshop on perennial forms, was that my deafness—or rather, the attitudes surrounding my deafness—were also a form of institutionalized religion. With that understanding I broke through—*really* broke through—to myself.

I've seen so many priests *say*—on the one hand—they'd love to have questions from us, but they *show* on the other hand that they'd rather not have to answer them. Speech therapists, audiologists, and teachers would rather not explain why sign language could be the best method with which to reach the minds of Deaf children; they simply told my parents that it would be bad for my speech. Did it ever cross Mom and Dad's minds that they would've learned a lot more from talking with other Deaf people? Sure, they knew many had gone downstate to the Michigan School for the Deaf in Flint, and they saw how different these children had seemed in the way they used their hands.

I honestly believe that if my parents were told that ASL would help my self-esteem and education, they would've learned it, along with my brothers and sisters, who would have probably picked it up more quickly than my parents. Almost every Deaf person I've met wished that their parents knew how to sign. Many of them have felt the frustration of wanting to communicate as easily as their hearing siblings, and yet they make do, either by mouthing and signing very slowly to their parents or writing notes back and forth on the kitchen table. I realize that I've been very fortunate to speak as clearly as I have, but that doesn't give me the right to gloat over any Deaf person's inability to articulate via speech. If any speech therapist was to point me out as an "oral success," I'd be the first to tell her that success does not listen to a perfectly enunciated word, but to the symphony of self-confidence. Speech never gave me the self-confidence with which to thrive; ASL did.

When one of my sisters emailed our family asking for sayings that we heard often while growing up, she was thinking of humorous quotes along the lines of "Quit throwing that ball in the house" and "Who are these kids, and why are they calling me Mom?" They would be incorporated into our upcoming family reunion's program book.

I would've liked to add a quote that I heard a lot when I couldn't follow the conversation around the dinner table: "I'll tell you later."

Of course, almost no one told me anything later. If I could earn a dollar for each time I heard that growing up, I'd have become a millionaire, but if I earned a dollar for each time someone actually told me later, I'd have remained dirt poor. Another quote whenever I followed up? "Not right now. I'm busy." Another? "Oh, gee, I forgot."

I had hoped that the passage of time, and educated enlightenment, would warm my siblings into welcoming me, a Deaf gay man, into their arms.

But it's become clear to me that their love for me is conditional. They'd love me more if I were straight, hearing, religious, apolitical (or at least Republican), and married with children. (Never mind the fact that I've accepted that they lead a "lifestyle" completely unlike my own, or that almost no one fingerspells even if I can't understand a particular word on the lips.)

The Deaf community doesn't seem to care about these kinds of expectations. They appreciate the unfiltered clarity of communication; this unifies us in spite of our many differences, whether they be political or not. They care, as much as I do, that we make an effort to make ourselves understood, and that's where the undeniable power of ASL comes in. It isn't just the compelling vision that soothes my eyes after speechreading; it's the sheer physicality of signing that makes me far more whole than the mere sensation of imperfect speech guttering out of my throat. One can hide behind wisps of words into the air with one's voice, but there is no ambush cover for hands conveying concepts in mere seconds. I love my hands because they can express my emotions far quicker, and more honestly, than mere spoken words can. Hearing friends inevitably remark on the dichotomy between my speaking and signing selves; they'd always thought that I was an animated talker, but no, I feel more emotionally in tune when I sign. Not worrying about the quality of my speech frees me to be more like my real self.

In 2009, when I was at the Rainbow Alliance of the Deaf conference in Chicago, I felt whole again. It didn't matter where each of us had originated from; what mattered was that we all wanted to be together—all 364 of us!—for a week. We understood what it felt like to be second-class citizens because we were Deaf, or because we were lesbian, gay, bisexual, transgender, queer/questioning, and other (LGBTQ+). The acceptance of each other among strangers and acquaintances felt far more unconditional than I'd felt from my own family. True family isn't about blood; it's understanding what is different from us so that we can better accept and love each other despite our many flaws. Second-class citizenship hurts, period. Love is a many-flavored picnic that would come up empty if it were limited to just the wine and cheese of speech and heterosexuality.

There is a saying that I'd longed to hear as a child but never did: "I'll tell you right now."

And, yes, you can quote me on that one.

——

During the 1970s, I *lived* for the Gogebic County Fair held every second weekend of August. None of us could wait to go there right after Dad came home from work that Thursday, so Mom and all of us nine kids piled into his mauve Pontiac station wagon. Dusk was approaching, a siren already calling her children of summer to autumn's impending curfew. We didn't care. We knew that a cacophony of blinking colored lights and a symphony of screams and pulsating music awaited us.

Held at the far edge of Ironwood, the fairgrounds were wedged next to the border of Wisconsin. Even from a distance, we could see the swaying seats of the Ferris wheel aching to rotate upward one more notch, and the soft explosion of colored lights below the wheel. Our excitement was impossible to contain in that station wagon.

Once Dad found a parking space, we flocked ahead to the pair of admission booths. I no longer remember how much it cost to get in, but my father was proud that all of us were there with him and Mom, especially if it was our neighbor Mrs. Lewinski working the booth.

After we slipped through the gate, Dad gave us money for the rides or whatever we wanted to do. This was a big deal because our weekly allowance was so small to begin with; I think we each got only fifty cents a week. We never thought of ourselves as poor, but we knew that some of our classmates had more money than we did.

With money in hand, we paired up in small groups and took off. I lingered behind with my younger sisters Andra and Vivien. Mom and Dad held their hands. They walked slowly to the white and green barns where the stench of manure and hay hit our nostrils. Still, I wanted to see how the cows and horses swatted at flies with their tails. They did this nonstop; it was as if their tails had their own brains. Most of them kept their faces away from us, seemingly annoyed with the strangers who filed through the aisles.

But I didn't have much patience for the 4-H animals. I wanted to go out to the midway and check out the rides. Every year, they were pretty much the same: Tilt-a-Whirl, Scrambler, and other rides with names I no longer recall. Andra and I rode together on these rides.

Andra and I played together a lot in the yard since Vivien was still so young. Vivien usually tagged along, especially when our older siblings began to break gradually from us. We were too young to run around the neighborhood by ourselves. Our world consisted of the woods across the street, our wide yards, and the vast playground at Norrie School a few blocks away. Andra was three years younger than me. She was always the one who'd instinctively understood that I needed help around the dinner table when it seemed like a room full of babble from kids vying for attention. She pointed out who was talking, and sometimes she mouthed to me what was being said. She usually sat across from me, next to our sister Jean.

Then she met her new best friend Julie, who lived a few blocks southwest of us. Andra soon developed what I thought was a strange hollow laugh. She worried more about what she was wearing. She didn't seem all that interested in helping me follow conversations around the dinner table anymore. I didn't quite understand what had happened or why, but I knew that Julie deserved to be hated. Maybe Andra had begun to see me through Julie's eyes. Having a deaf brother was strange and uncool. I will never know for sure, but the damage was done. She rarely talked to me again.

Still, in my memories of the Gogebic County Fair, Julie didn't exist, and if she had, I never sensed her presence in Andra when we went on those rides. It was as if we were close as before. Children have a way of neither caring that far into the future, nor dwelling on memories that would make adulthood a darker time of contemplation and regret. It was all about right now, right in this moment; so there we were, watching a gruffy, sweat-beaded, unshaven man with a cigarette hanging out of his mouth wobble the security latch in front of our feet and turn the ignition key for the first slow turn around the thick pole that held us a few feet off the trampled grass. In the short distance of shadows and flashing lights outside the fence that encircled us on the Scrambler, we could see Mom and Dad waving to us.

Sometimes they stood next to friends they knew or talked with customers that Dad knew from working the meat counter at Lopez's IGA off the highway. Dad was always pointing us out to people he knew. His wallet was thick with our latest school pictures, ready to be flashed to anyone who asked.

The Scrambler was a ride that spun around a pole, but in such a way that we were spun around invisible corners, so we were constantly squished together at these points. In between these sharp corners, we would separate and try to ignore the pain from the jabs of elbows and shoulders pushed against each other if one of us were caught on the wrong end. I didn't mind, because it was a physical closeness that I rarely got, more so when we grew older and distant. Once our spinning reached a crescendo of speed, our screaming and laughing and giggling hit a careless pitch. Our hands slid back and forth across the smooth metal bar in front of us. We stumbled out, full of giddiness and giggles.

The Tilt-a-Whirl was even better. We sat in a half-shell that spun around in circles at crazy angles as it groaned around a fat pole of blinking lights. The spinning was always staccato, a marriage of physics and machinery, so we never knew when we'd spin 360 degrees, or 180 degrees, swaying and waiting for the next shift in angle, for the reward of two full spins. Sometimes we got three spins. That nearly gave me a headache, but what a rush! We couldn't stop laughing. Things were all right again.

Since then, I have gone on numerous, and far more extreme, rides around the country at places like Cedar Point, Six Flags, and Valleyfair, but nothing can match the innocent exhilaration of letting go, welcoming the arms of gravity and allowing the endless screaming of delight and fear to begin all over again. There's truly nothing like the world we experience unchecked with our younger selves, not yet understanding how shallowness can encroach what used to be a closeness with someone you love. Nothing.

I've had many dreams of never speaking again. They recur whenever I recall my reactions to hearing my eight-year-old voice on a cassette tape from the winter of 1973, singing "Jingle Bells." I'd forgotten about the tape until Mom brought it out for me in the winter of 1991. I sat at the same kitchen table, remembering how Dad had recorded me, and listened to my voice after eighteen years. She smiled when she heard my voice and said, "That's really cute."

The fact that I sang it off-key didn't bother me, but hearing the tremulous labor in my voice to do it right—knowing that the tape recorder was running—and seeing her joyous reaction to the tape left me seething beyond words. She never had to endure hours and hours of mindless sound production like I had, so she listened to only what she wanted to hear. Those secret dreams of never speaking again returned to haunt me: this time, I wept happily. I *alone* had the power to decide how I wanted to communicate and to do whatever I wanted to do.

Oh, yes! Wherever I go, my hands—the truest home of my voice—will follow.

THE WORLD IS FULL OF ORPHANS

It's taken me years to articulate the defining fact of my childhood: I was an orphan. Wikipedia defines an orphan as "a child whose parents have died, are unknown, or have permanently *abandoned* them" (emphasis mine).

Growing up, I was shuttled between my biological family in Ironwood, Michigan, where there weren't educational facilities for deaf children like me, and Houghton, Michigan, a university town two hours away. Over a total of nine years, I lived with three different foster families in Houghton; I stayed with a foster family during the week, and with my biological family in Ironwood on weekends. (I also spent five years in a Catholic school system in Ironwood.)

I longed to fit in with my own hearing family, but in a small kitchen filled with eight siblings babbling all at once during mealtimes, it was next to impossible. I wasn't allowed to use ASL because it was believed that it would interfere with my speech therapy. If I wanted to know what was going on, the usual answer was, "I'll tell you later." Usually I would see them burst out laughing a few seconds after, forgetting that I was there. Of course, by the time the meal was over, they'd completely forgotten what was so funny.

I yearned for a world that made sense, a world where I could laugh as easily as they could without my straining to speechread.

I came to understand that if I complained about feeling left out, I'd be seen as a party pooper. I had to "toughen up." So if I did cry, it wasn't because I was feeling sorry for myself. It was because I couldn't articulate those feelings that came from not being included as an equal. I had no words for the loneliness that consumed me worse than paper on fire. I was the boy that no one wanted.

No one wants you if you're too different. In my case, I was both deaf and gay. I knew I was different, but I never questioned why I had to be punished for not hearing like everyone else. Somehow I'd intuited that if I did, I'd be even less popular. I followed the script of being the dutiful boy with clunky body hearing aids that operated out of a harness strapped to my chest, a boy who cleaned his entire plate while alternating between fanciful daydreams and foolish hopes that I'd someday be able to laugh along with everyone. In the world of my daydreams, I was king of all that happened. I became a storyteller without an audience.

Books were easy. They didn't require speechreading, or blast me with expressions of frustration if I asked them to repeat themselves, or mock me for not being able to understand dirty slang.

I read voraciously. Words, at first rising out of smoke and fog, began to lend weight to the dreams floating in and out of my head, giving me an unprecedented sense of control. When I read, I didn't have to be the deaf boy on the playground. I could be any character I wanted.

My oldest brother Mark gave me Meindert DeJong's novel *Hurry Home, Candy* one Christmas, and it became the very first book that I owned. (That it is about a stray dog with no name and no home of his own is eerily prescient, which is probably why I identified with it so strongly.) I read—and reread—that book. I felt as if I had a true friend who wouldn't hesitate to repeat stories until I understood each and every word. If I could count books as my friends, I had to be the most popular boy in school. The problem was, books just weren't cool.

The first time I had sex with a man happened in a library restroom. I was fourteen, and he was probably in his thirties. Even though I'd initiated it, I was still in shock afterward. This was something that wasn't in any book I'd read, and yet I knew I wanted more. He wasn't afraid of touching me; I wasn't an outcast. That was a new feeling.

I began to hunger for words about these experiences. My dreams became clearer. I didn't know what words could describe my ache for classmates my age and men I'd vaguely known, but my dreams were filled with them. I was in love so often that I was even afraid to say the word *love* to anyone. I was still the boy that my classmates shunted aside.

Being orphaned heightens doubts about one's place in the universe. If you don't have someone who loves you just as you are and who doesn't try to change you into something that you're not, you don't have a home of your own. It doesn't matter if you own a house. You're still lost.

Like any orphan, I knew that it would be a matter of time before I was chosen and whisked away to a good home. I waited and waited, with a library book in hand. Each time I read a book, I felt less like an orphan and more like a human being.

Once I arrived at Gallaudet in Washington, DC, in the summer of 1984, I soon realized that I didn't have to daydream anymore. I was suddenly among others of my kind, and they all used ASL. I didn't have to strain at lipreading or repeat myself if I'd mispronounced a phrase. What mattered was the clarity of our hands. Those of us with hearing families had experienced the pain of distance that made all of us orphans, and we were finally able to turn to each other for familial solace. We stayed up so many nights, just *signing*. We were truly home.

Lambda Rising, a LGBTQ+ bookstore off Dupont Circle, was my home away from Gallaudet. Sometimes I couldn't decide which were more enticing: the bearded men who prowled its aisles or the brand-new paperbacks that graced its shelves. Most of the time, the men didn't approach me, probably because they'd spotted the hearing aids behind my ears, but strangely enough, I didn't feel disappointed by their sudden loss of interest. A brand-new book was a more-than-adequate consolation prize.

With each purchase at Lambda Rising and at the nearby secondhand bookstore Second Story, I began to leave behind the world of mass-market paperbacks for trade paperbacks. I had discovered literature, and a whole new world of men whose words would nurture this writer into existence. Works like Christopher Isherwood's *A Single Man*, Oscar Wilde's *The Picture of Dorian Gray*, Edmund White's *A Boy's Own Story* and *States of Desire*, and Quentin Crisp's *The Naked Civil Servant* took me places, emotional and otherwise, that I hadn't known existed. Words weren't mere words anymore. They had *voices*. They were talking to *me*. They were telling me family stories as if I'd always been one of them. They never looked away from me as they carried on at the dinner table! I laughed and cried. And they never cared whether I was deaf or gay as long as I read. How I loved them all!

Then I happened to glance at a book—Charley Shively's *Calamus Lovers: Walt Whitman's Working-Class Camerados*—in Lambda Rising. A chapter described Mr. Whitman bathing naked with a younger Fred Vaughan in the East River off Brooklyn Heights, and even though the fantasy wasn't supported by historical documentation, I was struck by the eroticization of a writer in gay male terms. Of course, I'd read about gay sexual experiences before, but never those of an acclaimed writer in a description that mixed lust, love, and longing in equal measures by someone who'd never met him. It made me want Mr. Whitman, and I hadn't yet read *Leaves of Grass*! I'd never thought of writers, even though they talked about sex and its many incarnations in their work, as physically naked. Writers weren't just people who buttoned up their shirts, sat on a living room sofa, and talked to me about things after the fact. They were as full of yearning as I was.

Then I read the first edition of *Leaves of Grass*. I wasn't impressed. He seemed so full of babble. Nevertheless, whenever anyone talked about Mr. Whitman and his life, I paid attention. I learned more about him in bits and pieces. If I had read Gary Schmidgall's *Walt Whitman: A Gay Life* back then, I'd have become obsessed with him earlier. (Alas, that book didn't appear until a decade later.)

In the meantime, I came across Allen Ginsberg's poem "Howl." Blown away by his apocalyptic vision of America in the 1950s, I immediately thought of Walt Whitman. I read the second edition of *Leaves of Grass*, which many consider its best version, and I wept at his bucolic and sensuous visions. He wasn't afraid. Experiencing the love of his comrades in the purest form with true abandon had given him the strength and courage to celebrate all that was good—and bad—in life. It was also the first time where I'd seen how one writer could sire another. My English lit classes had of course discussed literary "influences," but I hadn't seen with my own eyes until that moment just how that was supposed to work.

Over the years, I've realized that Walt Whitman was a spectacularly virile man, inspiring one writer after another to celebrate the brotherhood of men in arms with their own kind. Although I don't write like him—nor would I dare to—I still count myself among his many sons. He continues to pat me on the shoulder at times when I feel my writing is going nowhere. He—along with the many writers who crowd my shelves—has given me what my own biological family has utterly failed to give me: the gift of encouragement to stay true to myself. Some years later, I would edit an anthology of queer male poetry in honor of the 200 years since Whitman's birth in 1819, and it was striking to see how many poets felt a sense of gratitude for not only Whitman, but also many others who'd followed in his footsteps.

When I was young, books at the Carnegie Public Library in Ironwood were just like people: mass-market thrillers with embossed titles and a whiff of danger belied the machismo of the yellowing acid-heavy pages as they lined up with their sagging spines. They were men who never stopped for a bathroom break. Romances were cleaner, filled with spiky curves that laced the titles. Women on the cover were always in a swoon over a man with a Tarzan-like physique, usually shirtless, hovering nearby if not actually cradling the woman in his strong arms. Once my sisters finished all the library's Barbara Cartlands, they moved on to consume the Harlequins on the lower rung of the romance food chain.

The shelves that bustled with torn cellophane and Dewey Decimal System numbers typed onto white square labels were like the stores that spread out down Aurora Street. Each place—Pamida, Johnson's Music Store, and Joe's Pasty Shop—had its own spines that pulled me closer each time I walked by. I never knew the people who stood behind the cash registers and washed the expansive windowpanes that stood guard between enticing merchandise and passersby, but each of their faces read as easily as the books

I borrowed. Each glance divulged the endings of their lives, and I knew instantly whether theirs was happy or not. Those with poker faces gave me pause, and I kept returning to them because they were books that wouldn't let me turn their pages at my usual pace. I had to keep rereading the lines on their faces for clues of foreshadowing. Sometimes I never learned their endings.

Each week when I went to the library, I checked the updated *New York Times* bestseller lists posted near the front desk. It was rather like watching the American Top 40 in slow-as-molasses motion, but it was always a thrill when a favorite author moved up a notch or two.

When I went to college in a city of over five million that was a thousand miles away, I began reading "literature." I was annoyed. Why did these dead writers have to seem so boring? Why did teachers have to dissect such ponderous prose that seemed to plop like manure right off the page? And what was so bad about reading better—and living—writers cranking out real page-turners? I dutifully speed-read the assigned tomes, but it still felt like the stump-hacking work I'd done one summer at the county fairgrounds.

The independent bookstores I began to browse were different from the B. Daltons in malls. They stocked trade paperbacks, which were then a new development in publishing. I came to adore these books because they combined the larger size of hardbound books and the cheaper price of paperbacks. Their elegant covers often revealed a quirky graphic design sensibility while sandwiching pages that didn't yellow as quickly as the mass-market paperbacks. I eventually realized that a far more vibrant intellectual and literary community existed beyond the *New York Times* bestseller list, but I still didn't see myself as worthy of their company. Their "literariness" seemed a bit too snooty for me.

Enter a creative writing teacher whom I'll call Ted. He was tall and bearded with piercing eyes and an easy laugh. He had written a much-celebrated short story that appeared in the *Atlantic Monthly* (now *The Atlantic*) and was subsequently published as one of the year's best stories in an anthology. In a workshop, he led us through our own short stories. His comments were always measured, thoughtful, and above all, encouraging.

I worshipped Ted from afar. He was a real writer who didn't have to call himself a writer. I hungered for him. I didn't dare reveal how much, and I was terrified of how much my eyes would reveal each time he saw me in class. I just couldn't cross that boundary between teacher and student. But at the semester's end, each of us students had to meet privately with Ted for a short discussion of our work. I showed up at his office, nervous and impatient with desire. I was about to graduate from college, and I was unsure where to go next. I had majored in English because I didn't know what else I wanted to do with my life. I still checked the *New York Times* bestseller lists regularly, and I swore that I would end up there myself one day. I would make a ton of money off my books.

Ted asked, "What kind of writer do you want to be?"

"I don't know."

"Literature is better."

As I gazed up into his eyes, he smiled ever so kindly.

I wanted to kiss him right there, but I chickened out.

In that moment of insecurity, my journey as a writer had truly begun. I discovered Penguin Classics, literary fiction, and poetry on my own. My writing began to shed its smug glibness and coy forced cleverness, and it wasn't long before one of my pieces scored a major magazine cover. The writers I once disparaged in college watch over my shoulder now as I write.

It's impossible to choose only one influence as my singular inspiration as a gay writer. In this, I'm blessed to have such a loving family reunion each time I browse my bookcases.

I am the son of many fathers who've inspired me with their words and actions, and I hope to honor their legacy with my craftsmanship. I hope to sire others wise enough to know that our ancestors were far greater than I can ever hope to be. I am nothing without them.

Thus, it has recently occurred to me that I'd never really been alone while growing up. Books were my first true family. Whenever a book of mine is published, I release it out into the world, trusting that at least one kind-hearted stranger will adopt it and cherish it as much as I have. People come to my readings, often to tell me how they've enjoyed this or that book of mine. In fact, two hearing poets told me recently that they've reread my collection *Mute* front to back at least three times. This fact touches me deeply more than they'll ever know: it means that I've become family to someone who's chosen to listen. Such are my proudest moments as a father.

The world is full of orphans, and yet how heartening it is to see that, among books, one is never alone!

MY FRIENDSHIP WITH LONELINESS

On some mornings, when I pause to look at my middle-aged self in the mirror, I am struck by how much I've changed since the days I spent standing by the brick walls of Ironwood Catholic Grade School watching my hearing classmates play Nerf football.

They called me the runt of the class and made me the brunt of their cruel jokes.

I was not only the *only* deaf child in my family of nine children but also the *only* deaf child I knew of in my hometown of some 6,000 people. It didn't help that I had to wrestle with doubts over my growing sexual attraction to men. And my family didn't encourage talking about feelings.

I had become mute in more ways than one. I could speak well enough to be understood in class, but I had no vocabulary for the differentness that gnawed at me from within.

I could lipread well enough to follow most teachers in class, but I had no friends to make me feel like a part of their world.

I had to sit in the front row in order to lipread the teacher, which meant two things: the teacher would keep an eye on me, and the popular kids sitting in the back would watch me and snicker.

I waited and waited while my ears seemed to become me and nothing else. I felt at times that I was born to hide and wait.

But waiting for what?

I still had no words for what I wanted, but I knew it had to be more than wanting to have a friend to call my own.

Loneliness was my best friend in those days. He slept with me, his arms holding me tight and his face breathing inchoate dreams into my waiting head. I made love to Loneliness, but he didn't want me. He wasn't in love with me. He hurt my feelings because if Loneliness, that runt of all human life, didn't want me, who else did?

I was so ready for anything, but I didn't know what *anything* was.

My parents didn't want me to learn sign language. They were told that it would interfere with my speech. There was an older Deaf man in town who was a high school dropout and who washed dishes at the local Holiday Inn outside town, but I was forbidden to interact with him.

I was fourteen the summer when I finally dared to make my way, unannounced, to that Deaf man sitting outside a tavern. He lit up when he saw me approaching him; he'd apparently heard about me from others, so he beckoned me to sit down on his bench. I didn't know what I was looking for, but I'd somehow sensed that his hands held the key to my happiness. He showed me how to fingerspell, and how to look into each other's eyes, not at each other's hands while signing.

My parents were very displeased, but like most parents, they'd forgotten what it felt like to be a child growing up and wanting to explore the world. They also often forget that puberty is an awkward time of sexual awakening, and they seldom dared discuss it with their children.

Eventually, I asked to transfer back to Houghton High School two hours away where there was a program that used sign language as a mode of instruction. There, I had some deaf friends, but they, too, hadn't learned the language of being happy with their own deafness. I felt something missing, but I had no words for it.

Being a student at a Deaf university changed my life completely. It was the last time I saw my old friend Loneliness, and it was the first time I knew fully what I wanted from my life. I wanted never to be ashamed of what I was and to make friends with people who would accept me as I am, as I had accepted myself. My hands had become alive with language and love. I was no longer that skinny boy standing by the brick walls of Ironwood Catholic Grade School, wishing to hear as well as everyone else.

I've learned that when I allow myself to be different instead of trying to conform all the time, I have a good deal more energy for the more important things in my life. I love my own deafness. I love the fact that it makes me far more different as a person than if had I stayed hearing. I love the fact that I'm immediately much more at home with a Deaf stranger than with a hearing stranger because that experience of growing different bonds us immediately in ways that very few hearing people can understand. I love the fact that it's given me the power of heartfelt appreciation of a language that's continued to defy oppression for generations. When I am told to speak even when it's far too difficult for a person to understand me in the middle of a noisy bar, I learn to find new ways of expressing myself through my hands.

I love my own gayness. I love the fact that it makes me far more open to the fluid spectrum of sexuality. I love the fact that it has enabled me to stop judging others—straight and otherwise—who might get off on kink and otherwise. I love the fact that being gay means embracing the very gray area of sexuality itself, which can be monogamous, open, or polyamorous; this freaks out many heterosexuals raised on a black-and-white view of their sexuality, making no separation between love and lust. When a straight person tells me I cannot kiss another man on the street, I learn to kiss fear on the lips.

I'm glad to have made friends with Loneliness. He's taught me many things, but above all, he gave me the strength and stamina to believe myself worthy of love and acceptance. I still say hello to him from time to time, for even Loneliness needs a little love and acceptance, too.

YOU'RE TOO OLD FOR ME

"You're too old for me."

A man in his late twenties with whom I'd been chatting online felt it was his duty to inform me that because I was forty years old, I was "not a good match." It didn't matter that my profile had stated that I was looking only for friends as I'd just moved into a new city. That was my first shock of realization that I'd somehow crossed the invisible boundary between young and . . . "old." I was already "too old" at forty? Whoa.

This was a new kind of rejection. I had often been rejected because of my deafness. It didn't matter if I was a very good lipreader, wore hearing aids, and could speak rather intelligibly. For years I used to chalk such rejections up to ignorance, but ever since the internet came to the fore as a way of meeting prospective partners instead of through personal ads in the back of print periodicals, something else became quite transparent.

Imagine what goes on during a Saturday night in a typical gay neighborhood bar. Regulars catch up on the latest in their own lives. The muscular and shirtless A-listers nurture their drinks and do not look at men who do not meet their criteria—not buff enough, not tall enough, not clean-shaven, not fashion-forward, not tanned enough, not whatever. Now imagine that same bar multiplied thousands and thousands of times over in size, but which seems more like a bathhouse with everyone wearing the masks of A-listers constantly practicing the cutting art of rejection on each other even though their flabby bellies, drugstore glasses, and Wal-Mart clothes give them away once they open their towels around their waists. That is what the internet sometimes feels like when it comes to gay dating. You are already rejected before you even open your mouth to say hello. Just a little *something* somewhere in your profile was apparently too much. It's no accident that many profiles do not reveal much, and I don't think that those are all closet cases seeking discreet sex. They've gotten tired of the rejection. When a vast number of bathhouses shut down during the 1980s due to the hysteria over the AIDS epidemic, something similar had to take its place. It wasn't long before the internet became *the* bathhouse of choice. While the internet's vast size alone has made it possible for us to seek out those who may share in some of our more peculiar sexual proclivities and fantasies, something's been lost in that transition from trying to make eye contact with people in bars, coffeehouses, and bookstores (pre-"real-time") to chatting with people online before finally meeting for a cup of coffee or a lusty hookup ("real-time"). While searching online, we dream so constantly of our perfect partner that when we do meet someone who's a little different, we reject him outright without giving him a chance. And naturally, most hearing people do not dream of having a Deaf partner. They dream of being able to whisper sweet nothings in bed, calling each other on the phone, and watching the latest Hollywood blockbuster at the cineplex. If I were a muscular hunk with a V-shaped chest and a six-pack stomach, I'd still ultimately get rejected. Hearing aids or imperfect speech can be a major problem at dinner parties where simultaneous conversations and spontaneous jokes can flit around the table. Deafness is too much of a hassle for them.

When people enter a relationship, they know they have to make compromises. But for some reason, accommodation for a physical need isn't seen in quite the same light. Deafness—well, *any* form of disability, for that matter—isn't A-list material. But neither is "old." I read somewhere years ago that all of us will eventually experience disability in some form over the course of our lives. This could mean recuperating from a car accident, battling a bout of chronic depression, and so on. Despite such exposure to these experiences, we still *fear*. It still doesn't matter when we hear Franklin Delano Roosevelt say, "The only thing we have to fear is fear itself." We so do *not* want to be disabled; therefore, we are in the habit of avoiding other disabled people as if their wheelchairs and canes and spastic muscle movements are contagious. And we do not want to be seen as old therefore we avoid talk of our mortality and the bodies of our elders. Their tan liver spots and double chins might be contagious. Well, you never know!

There is also that guilt by association. When was the last time you saw an A-lister chatting with a man in a wheelchair in public? Disability taints. If we hang around with people with disabilities in public, we are finally admitting to the world that we are not A-listers, instead of pretending that we're too cool for anyone but ourselves. Yayyy—we're officially losers.

Rejection sucks. But I've learned that it's more effective to be upfront in my profile than to slip in a zinger late in our first online chat: "Oh, btw, I'm Deaf." If they can't deal with the very idea of my deafness in spite of what I have to offer, they are *so* not for me. But if they are intrigued anyway, chances are *very* good that they are not intimidated by the many challenges that life throws them. That is the best kind of friend anyone would want. I have made good friendships this way.

The best thing about disability—or aging, for that matter—is that those who are willing to look past these things tend to be *very* genuine. They're not the shallow ones. They're not afraid of what is different about us. They're the ones who seek out new experiences and friendships. And if they actually are attracted to us because we *are* disabled and/or old, which gives them a window into their own experiences, more power to them. We have long battled the impossible standards of beauty, and attitudes that reflect anything different from these norms is a welcome wind of change. Physical beauty needs to take on many forms in our lives in order for us—whether disabled, older, or not—to feel truly beautiful. Ugliness is indeed beautiful because without such ugliness, we have no other way of appreciating beauty. We must learn to see beauty in ugliness and ugliness in beauty. As George Michael once sang, "Don't you think I'm looking older? / But something good has happened to me."

Many people think deafness has made my life difficult. Yes, but never in the way they think it does. When I am alone, or when I'm signing with a Deaf friend, I don't feel disabled. The attitudes and ignorance of the hearing world are far more disabling than anything else in my life. They shout their conversations at me when I don't need the volume. They want to learn dirty signs and laugh without wanting to know me as a person. They shout right into my hearing aid when I get more out of lipreading them, particularly in a noisy bar. They do not see the point of learning ASL because if I can lipread and talk, why bother? They do not understand that lipreading is a very inexact art, or that hands are much easier to *see*. And some of them seem to think that deafness equals stupidity.

The baby boomers, through their sheer force of numbers, have caused enormous social upheavals from the mid-1940s and on. They have led the way for the countercultural revolution, the gay liberation movement, the women's rights movement, and so on. As the aging LGBTQ+ baby boomers continue to make their needs felt in their communities, I know that their old ideas of youth and perfection—crafted by endless days in gyms and shown off in bars and discos of long ago—will simply have to fall away, if it hasn't happened already. The existence and recognition of a bear community in the late 1980s and early 1990s were only a foretaste of what was to come. Suddenly it was *okay* to desire men who weren't lithe twinks, and to be desired for a little heft. A little hairy belly could be considered hot, and the salt in a salt-and-pepper moustache was suddenly a virtue.

I have seen online ads looking specifically for men *their* age and older. I remember trying once to get my mind around the very concept of a sixty-year-old man wanting a partner in his seventies. I thought, "Gee, that's *old!*" and then I caught myself. *I* am "old." Yet the funny thing about aging is that it doesn't start at the age of forty. It starts the second we are born. Our A-list attitudes just haven't aged fast enough.

And what did I say to that immature twentysomething who informed me that I was "too old"? "Oh, sorry. I didn't realize I was too young for you."

HANDS, ROMANCING

The twinkle in his eyes shone in the picture above his online profile. More clicked pictures revealed a tall and fit man with a graying trimmed beard standing astride his bicycle, smiling next to his children, and smooching a close female friend. Hmm. I had long been used to the lack of responses to my emails expressing interest, so I thought, what the heck.

I sent him an email with a link to my profile that indicated my deafness and my feelings about the bar scene (usually too dark to lipread and too loud to hear anyone even with my residual hearing). Within minutes, we were chatting online. We talked about our lives. He had raised three children and was living with two of them, now nearing the end of their high school years. I had moved to Minneapolis the year before after having lived in New York for seventeen years. He was happily divorced. I had been in a fifteen-year relationship that ended amicably. He shared his Jungian perspective on life. I was intrigued, more so because he knew ASL and understood Deaf culture. It was an odd yet thrilling experience to find a hearing person teasing me about being Deaf; he was respectful with his inside knowledge.

Our first date a few days later in an Italian gourmet comfort café was awkward at best. We were both guarded, unsure about each other, even as our voiceless hands conveyed volumes about ourselves. Yet the weight of unspoken expectations seemed to color the Wednesday lunch atmosphere gray as if to complement the overcast clouds. We walked around my neighborhood and talked housing prices. He was in the market to buy a house after years of living in rented apartments and houses and taking care of his children. He was looking forward to having his own freedom back once his kids left the nest. When we arrived at his car, he seemed to tower over me as he stroked my arm almost without warning, right there on Hennepin Avenue. He was two inches taller than I was, and I could not help but look up into his gray eyes. He gave me a smile so gentle and unexpected. I was quite taken aback by the tenderness in his hands as he touched me goodbye. I agreed to meet him again.

Two days later, we biked around the nearby Cedar Lake. But first, we went to a food co-op, bought ourselves lunch, and loaded the food up on his bike. As I watched him coast down the paved path winding around the lake, I was taken by the smooth beauty and shape of his shirtless back. He was justifiably proud of his chest. The more we biked, the more he began to flirt. He wriggled his ass at me and made some sly comments about my body as he suddenly sailed by. He knew that most hearing people wouldn't know what he said in ASL, so it was like a secret language that only we knew.

The flirtations were intoxicating. Here I was, already forty years old, and it hit me that no one had tried to flirt with me so incessantly, and quite so openly. It seemed that dates consisted of two events (meeting and having sex), but here I was, in the limbo-land between meeting and conjugating. Sometimes we stopped and ate part of our picnic before we moved on to the next lake. All told, we ended up going around three lakes and learning more about each other than we ever could had we stayed in restaurants each time we met.

Then we biked past Lake Bde Maka Ska, which often boasted an ongoing parade of lookers and onlookers usually wearing the ubiquitous white iPod earbuds while on foot, rollerblades, and bikes.

Up the hill we climbed toward Lake Harriet. I saw how the unexpected sun cast a glint of glare in the rivulets of sweat winding down his back. Then down and around the lake, we wove under the hanging trees until we stopped at the bandstand.

No one sat on the stage, so we ate ice cream and melded our hands. I told him more than I'd told most people, and he told me more than I'd expected to hear. Family dynamics in our pasts had shaped us differently for different reasons, but I understood his frustrations. I was surprised when he opened my legs on the edge of the stage and pulled me closer to him for a kiss.

I was surprised by his need, and I still hadn't finished my ice cream!

I was used to being discreet with my desire for another in public, especially now that I was no longer living in the more gay-friendly Manhattan. I was floored by his flattery.

By the time it was time for us to part, six hours had passed. I felt giddy when I saw him leave with his bike hitched to the back of his car. What had I missed from all those years when I was single and dating? A giggly lightheadedness that I didn't think was quite possible. I was forty years old, for God's sake!

A few days later, he showed up at my apartment for dinner. We didn't say a word as he crossed the threshold into my arms. We embraced for a few minutes, and in that fleeting moment, I closed my eyes and inhaled the scent of his cologne-free neck. I felt his pulse throb slightly against my chin and the smooth inclines of his back. I thought nothing but the sweet musk of his smell wafting deeply into my brain and down into my groin.

As much as I hadn't wanted to, I finally broke away. The logistics of cooking my first meal for him had encroached on my mind: heat up the electric stove top, take out the pair of tuna steaks, toss a few drops of toasted sesame oil and some beef broth into the pan, along with some pimentos and capers. Simple, perhaps, but incredibly effective as a quick dinner.

After we ate, he said, "That was good. You didn't hold back anything. Let's do it again."

We hugged, this time for longer. I've hugged all my boyfriends and partners, but never as long as I did with him while standing there, so still as time itself. I felt bathed in that warm light emanating from the kitchen table. The world was full of shadow, but there he stood like a beacon in my arms. I looked up at him, and we kissed. Simply and lightly.

We smiled quietly at each other. There was absolutely no pressure to do more than leave a lingering mark on each other's lips.

He kicked off his sandals and walked barefoot across the carpet to my leather loveseat.

I brought out a small bowl containing Kalamata olives, heated in two quick turns in my microwave oven, and an empty ramekin for the pits. I placed them on the coffee table in front of my loveseat. He sat down on one end as I placed a warm olive into his mouth. His lips pursed around my fingertips as he looked up into my eyes. His eyes widened at the burst of unexpectedly strong olive flavors on his tongue, and then he grinned. I held the ramekin in front of him where he let the pit drop from his mouth. He beckoned for another olive, and as he took it with his teeth, his tongue suddenly darted out to lick my fingertips. His eyes never strayed from mine as his tender taste buds curled around the pistils of my hands opening up like a flower.

I leaned down and kissed him.

He lathered my tongue with olives that grew in Spain and were imported to a local shop near my home. His tongue was a foreign country with unfamiliar scents, quite different from the waft of his neck earlier.

He broke the kiss, spit out the pit, and brought a fresh olive up to my lips. This I took with my teeth, and I expertly bit its purple flesh off the stone pit. I let it fall out of my mouth into the ramekin, and our tongues danced a tango as arms melded around bodies on the sofa. The olive finally consumed, I rested lightly atop his chest and closed my eyes. I imagined that I was outside somewhere under an olive tree, even though I'd yet to see one in my life. His hands slid slowly around the contours of my back as I sensed his sighing.

The reality of our crampedness on the loveseat finally broke our spell.

I guided myself off him and realized that I'd forgotten to do one other thing. I plugged in the white Christmas lights that I'd left hanging all around my four windows. He took off his shirt without any ado and lay there, his face softly lit, and his eyes were almost as bright. I fed him another olive, and while we signed to each other, we took turns feeding each other the ever-cooling olives still seeped in their juices.

Sips from our glasses of ice-laden water refreshed our moods as we chatted between eating a chopped green pepper, which I had wanted to use up as it wouldn't belong in the salad I was to make.

The sudden crunchiness of cool pepper was a contrast to the warm tanginess of olive. As I sat there admiring his chest, I found his hand holding my left as I signed with my right hand. Even though ASL usually requires both hands for unencumbered communication, context often enables the other person to fill in mentally the other half of the two-handed signs used when one hand is occupied with something else. He understood me perfectly.

A dream had come true, hadn't it? A handsome hearing man could understand me perfectly without the need to use my voice, and he was so fluent in ASL that I didn't need to use both hands to be understood! There weren't many of those out there.

As I chopped up shallots and whirred a blend of olive oil and balsamic vinegar in a mini food processor to create the salad dressing in the kitchen, he took my salad spinner and spun its wet greens so much that each leaf bounced to the bottom of the colander with a springiness. I showed him where he could mix the greens and other ingredients before he poured the dressing.

He knew how much I couldn't get enough of his naked chest, so he took every opportunity to rub his pectorals across my back or lean against the cupboard above the sink while he watched me sear the sashimi-quality tuna steaks quickly into a pastel brown with their centers quite pink. His half-naked body distracted me, but I managed to pour the pan sauces over both of our plates as he sat down at the table. I felt secretly proud of not having made a cooking mistake thus far, and of being able to put together a decent meal even on a dinner date. As we ate, we held hands across the narrow table as a singular lamp shone on our food and lent a soft glow on our faces.

No one asked to take an instant photograph of us.

No one offered us roses for sale.

No one sang an Italian aria before our table.

All that silence was quite alright with us.

As we ate, we signed and smiled and stared into each other's eyes. The world, however small it had been in our hands that moment, was fleetingly ours that night, that gem-like transcendence of memory forever mine. That night, our hands spoke louder than words.

IS GAYNESS A DISABILITY?

"I'm gay and I consider homosexuality a disability." This statement comes from a student playwright who won an award for his play about a character with a mental illness. (I will not name him, but I will quote him directly.) "I'm physically programmed to want things I can't have. Ninety-five percent of the men I'm attracted to are physically incapable of reciprocating. It's not a matter of taste or even a social or cultural issue. It's a biological disaster of circumstance, and to me that's a disability."

As a Deaf gay man, I was both provoked and offended by his remarks.

My electronic version of *The Webster's Revised Unabridged Dictionary*, interestingly, presents both definitions of *inability* and *disability* at the same time: "Inability is an inherent want of power to perform the thing in question; disability arises from some deprivation or loss of the needed competency." By this definition, in his pursuit of (presumably) heterosexual men, he suffers from the *inability* to find a reciprocal relationship, which is something many people suffer from regardless of sexual orientation; it's called "unrequited love." We have all experienced the pangs of being unwanted by the ones we wanted, but we eventually overcome those feelings and move on to more fulfilling relationships.

Looking again at the definition of *disability* in terms of homosexuality, it appears that he, unfortunately, sees himself as beneath—not equal to—heterosexuals because he cannot have the men he wants, as in "deprivation or loss of the needed competency." If I'd seen myself as somehow inferior to my straight counterparts when I was 18 years old (his age at the time), I wouldn't have had the guts to come out thirty-six years ago at Gallaudet at a time when it wasn't the thing to do. I knew that I deserved equal footing with everyone else, not because I had delusions of self-entitlement, but because I knew that above all, I was a human being like everyone else. If we in the LGBTQ+ community thought of ourselves as second-class citizens, we certainly wouldn't have made such incredible—and happily visible—progress in our pursuit of equal rights since the Stonewall Riots. That anyone as young as him still feels that he is "disabled" *today* is very sad, to say the least. Such internalization means that we still have a very long battle in overcoming homophobia among the young, in spite of the growing number of positive and well-rounded portrayals of LGBTQ+ characters in television, film, literature, and theater. A straight man in an all-gay milieu might feel himself to be "gay-impaired," but I doubt he'd feel disabled because of his desire for a woman; he'd simply seek out places where he could meet straight women. His "disability" would disappear immediately in the same way that my own disability would if I were among a group of signers. Gay men often congregate to reaffirm that it is okay to be who they are in a world that doesn't want their openness. I don't blame them. My own family, as much as they love me, would prefer that I be married to a woman and raising children!

But the student playwright didn't say specifically whether he is attracted to straight men, or indeed, men of a certain physical type; however, I wonder how he knows that the "ninety-five percent" of the men he desires "are *physically incapable of reciprocating*" [italics added for emphasis]. It is possible that some of these men are in the closet. It is also possible that some of them, while gay, do not feel attracted to him, but I wouldn't consider them "physically incapable of reciprocating." And if impotence happens, it's not caused by sexual orientation. If he truly feels "disabled," I would strongly suggest that he go to places where gay men congregate in the same way a straight man seeking to meet other straight women would go, such as a singles event.

Even though I'm Deaf, I don't see myself as deprived in any way, even though I may not be able to hear everything. Yes, technically, I do have a disability in the eyes of the hearing world, which can be an occasional problem, but over the course of my life as a Deaf person since losing my hearing at the age of eight months, I've come to see that *attitudes* of the hearing world are much more of a disability than my own. Many hearing people babble on and do *not* listen to each other; but I, as a Deaf person, *do* listen to each hearing person I communicate with even if it means struggling to speechread in a dim restaurant.

Hearing people, whether they realize it or not, *need* Deaf people as a constant reminder of the inestimable importance of clear, unfettered communication in the same way that straight people *need* gay people as a constant reminder of the need for tolerance of all forms of sexual desire. It's no accident that ASL is so cherished within the Deaf community: Hands are a lot easier to read than lips, tongue, and throat, and are a lot less misunderstood. By the same token, it's no accident that many gay visitors in a new locale often immediately want to know where they can find others of their kind. Regardless of disability, sexual orientation, creed, race, and all the other elements in lives lived that make each person so endlessly fascinating, we are social creatures in constant need of acceptance and love by those who do understand our way of life.

Merriam-Webster's dictionary gives an additional clarification of the word *disability*: "The condition of being unable to perform as a consequence of physical or mental illness." Just how is sexual desire for one's own gender a disability here? Gay people would insist that they are as capable as anyone in their day-to-day functioning, just as many disabled people are as capable as anyone in their day-to-day functioning, as long as accommodations such as ramps and assistive listening devices are made. Reinforcement of our positive self-image of ourselves as a vibrant and diverse group of people with dreams and hopes as real as the boy or girl—or even those who are nonbinary or trans—next door is the best cure against the disability of homophobia.

TO LOSE IS TO LIVE

Half a lifetime ago, I lived in New York. I didn't know then what I was looking for, except that I wanted to be there, the maelstrom that was Manhattan, the birthplace of so many heroes who'd inspired me to read, reconsider, rewrite. There, in my tiny room in a fifth-floor walkup off the corner of West Fourth and West Tenth Streets, a block away from the heart of Greenwich Village otherwise known as the intersection of Christopher Street and Seventh Avenue South, I sat on a stool and wrote on a twelve-pound Zenith laptop that ran MS-DOS and WordPerfect off two disk drives; no hard drive. In those days, when I wrote my Deaf gay novel, I wore headphones and played Suzanne Vega's *Days of Open Hand* nonstop on my CD player. Even though I cannot always hear the music fully, I imagined the music containing a twinge of melancholy, a sense of yearning to break free but feeling unable to.

Each time I hear Suzanne Vega's "Men in a War" or "Rusted Pipe," forgotten details of the late 1980s and early 1990s always come back to me in a rush.

I'm old enough to recall reading about GRID, the acronym for Gay-Related Immune Deficiency. I was a senior in high school, and I knew I was gay, and here, a national news magazine was telling me that there was a mysterious disease seemingly wiping out only gay men by the hundreds?

I didn't know then that reading the article was my first taste of loss as a gay man. I didn't know that I would read stories about men sucking and fucking indiscriminately anywhere they could in large cities like New York and San Francisco, and also long for that sense of uninhibited freedom. I didn't know that I would later meet Deaf gay men like myself, only to find out that one by one they'd die. In the historical footage of my hospital visits with these men that still replays from time to time in my dreams, I watch them signing to me. It's not their pallid faces pockmarked with Kaposi's sarcoma; it's the thinness of their wrists that stops me. How was it possible that their limbs could turn into toothpicks? Their fingers took longer to sign, and then, with a tired look of surrender in their eyes, they turned their heads away and released their final breath.

I was frightened; so much so that when I moved to New York in September 1988, I was wary of having sex with anyone. No exchange of bodily fluids; not even saliva. My fantasies were all shrink-wrapped in cellophane.

In that tiny room that had no air conditioner, I sweated and wrote profusely in the summer of 1990. I never forgot their stories of what it was like to be Deaf gay men during the halcyon freewheeling days of the 1970s. I wanted somehow to make it possible for others to remember them as I had. With each Deaf gay friend who died, I pushed myself harder to write, to finish. I wrote hundreds of pages not out of blind grief, but out of my dogged determination not to forget the firefly impressions of the Deaf men I'd met in San Francisco, New York, and Washington, DC.

I didn't know it then, but I was creating my first scrapbook featuring a family I so loved, cherished, and still miss. Focusing on their stories forced me to live more fully on the page. I would do things that I couldn't have had the gumption to do in the nerve-wracking climate of AIDS hysteria and fear. I would pretend to be one of those hot Deaf guys who fucked one hearing man after another in the dark labyrinth of a bathhouse. Out by the West Side Highway, I would trick with nameless strangers with not an iota of fear at all.

When they told me one story after another in the bars where we convened, they were acknowledging to me that I was one of them, that I was family. The language of hands that we shared had automatically made me so. Even if I'd known them for a fleeting moment, they told me that I was beautiful; not in the way that I looked then, but from the fact of my fluency in ASL, I understood what they'd conveyed. I felt accepted, loved. They told me firsthand stories about hearing teachers and speech therapists who had tried their damnedest to eradicate ASL to the point of tying their hands behind their backs. They would make them speak, Goddammit! They had to speak! Speak. SPEAK! They had to be like hearing people! Oh, yes, they would *conform.*

If only a portable video camera were as affordable then!

Today the internet is filled with clips of Deaf people signing, vlogging, and performing in ASL and other foreign sign languages from all over the world. The ghosts of these Deaf men would've stared slack-jawed at the sheer multitude of all those videos. They would've wept.

Some nights when I needed a break from my writing, I strolled around the Village and wondered about the mysterious lives behind the windows and doors of the houses and apartment buildings nearby. Who were these people? They were like shadows to me.

Each time I return to New York, I am always struck by how familiar yet strange my old neighborhood feels. Had I truly lived here? Or was it only a dream so vivid I'd have sworn it did happen?

But I do know that it wasn't a dream. No matter where I am in the Village, my feet know where to go. My heart is a compass. The ghost of my youth is always waiting for me around the next corner. The city may change, but the ghost of my youth will always stay forever young.

I write because I'm mindful that people get rejected every day even within their own families. The outcasts, the misfits, the unwanted. I want to set down stories and say, *This is what it was like before you came along. This is your true family history. You will become magnificent as the sun.*

One day I too will become forgotten; perhaps a footnote wedged in someone's bibliography if I'm that lucky. We are literally made of the same elements as stars, so to that great sky of mystery and shadow we shall return. We shall glitter and inspire.

———

In 1927, the astronomer Arthur Eddington developed a concept known as "the arrow of time." He figured that time itself went one way only; in other words, there was no symmetry when it came to how the universe unfolded. The universe has a built-in date of expiration; some have estimated that the sun won't truly die out for at least a few billion years. To think in smaller terms, the hard shells of a seed when it splinters in the spring, won't become the seed it was before. The shells will decompose right back into the soil. The seed goes through time in one direction only.

Everything will eventually fade. *Everything.*

If that's the case, why bother to create anything? To remember?

If we can leave behind a record of how we'd lived and loved, we have a much better chance of turning our own arrows of time into something akin to the spears of time. We will last a few moments longer and land with a greater impact.

To lose is to gain something in its place. Sometimes it's not what you want, and sometimes it's not readily apparent. But it is there, even if it's just an idle memory.

So aim your bow and let the arrow land where it must.

I haven't read my Deaf gay novel since its publication in 2009. I cannot read it again because it will make me so sad, recalling the original flickers of light inherent in their hands. Life is like that. A firefly flame, and then it's gone. The echo of night is all we have.

But the heart is a video camera. It's constantly recording, and therefore it does remember, much like how hearing a certain song will unexpectedly bring back the footage you'd completely forgotten. It is then you realize how much you'd truly lived, and how much more you need to live.

In each of us is a brilliant nebula.

Explode.

Seriously. Do not be afraid to detonate. Time is an arrow still sailing through the air.

Oh, do spread your wings. Your hearts are covered with Plexiglas feathers, and you will astound others when you flap your wings, shocking everyone who thought you couldn't fly. You are a neon swan.

Shimmer.

The fallout is pure elegy. It is the residue of art. The one feather of yours that survives long enough to float down to the ground is everyone's memento. It will twinkle into many feathers worn as a badge of pride.

Fade.

Horrible to do, but necessary. Take your place among the stars, the ultimate dream factory.

To lose is to live on in everyone's dreams among the stars.

DREAMING DIFFERENTLY

I remember the first time I saw Manhattan itself: not the grungy subway that hurtled me and my friends from Kings Highway in Brooklyn on a spring break visit from Gallaudet, not the stench of piss and rancid French fries, not the bored looks of people riding the train, but the moment of blue sky opening folds of shadows, prying apart cluttered buildings, to reveal a particular building in the distance from the corner of Sixth Avenue and West Fourth Street, when we turned the corner from the West Fourth subway exit and climbed onto the gum-blackened sidewalks. There, in the sliver of trees and sky ahead, I saw that building, a glimmer of hope, of possibility; not sure why it grabbed my attention the way it had. Little did I know that I would end up living in that very building three years later. Manhattan, as it did then and still does now whenever I visit, swirled around and all over me with its kinetic, frenetic energy; I saw fashion trends unthinkable then in the staid byways of Washington, DC, where I was attending college. The year was 1986, and I wasn't even twenty-one. But, like the brilliant raconteur Quentin Crisp later told me, "When I saw New York, I wanted it."

I was full of dreams then. I consumed bestsellers by Jay McInerney, Tama Janowitz, and Bret Easton Ellis; delved into the minimalist fictions of Amy Hempel, Raymond Carver, and Grace Paley; even subscribed to *The Village Voice*, its weekly issue rolled tightly into my mailbox at Gallaudet. I learned its history, the bewildering tableaux of beautiful and talented ones broken too easily by the city, turned into legends. George Plimpton's book about Edie Sedgwick lit a window into the heady days of Andy Warhol's Factory days, and how people fluttering around wanted fame, did almost anything for a moment in the spotlight. Then I saw Woody Allen's film *Hannah and Her Sisters* by happenstance on a friend's television; I had never seen a film structured like that, a story weaving in and out of each character's life, echoing and reacting. New York, oh New York: such a different, intoxicating world! I longed to live among its millions; the romance, the excitement was irresistible to someone like me, a young writer with ambition to burn.

How little did I know that New York would try to break me so relentlessly. It's not a city for dreamers with thin skins. Everywhere an unexpected glance can be sharp as a shard, pierce the heart of your dreams, the sacrosanct place where you'd worked so hard on your writing; doesn't matter as long as it's your art. You've lived it, bled it, and put it out there in hopes that others will see how much of you is good, that you are indeed talented. You will constantly learn that no matter how hard you rewrite, your work will never be good enough; mostly shit. Agents, editors, and publishers won't want it. Everyone will always look for the tiniest reason to reject you.

I was honestly amazed at the kind of writing that got published and promoted on the tables and shelves in Barnes & Noble, for it wasn't always that good. What mattered was that you had to know *somebody* with some pull. A little talent coupled with discipline is always helpful, but if you knew someone, or a close friend willing to recommend her agent to you, or if your parents had grown up with that agent—well, you had a tiny chance at scoring a little recognition, admittedly a vast feat in a city of over eight million people. I've certainly tried.

Then a little thing called the internet came in and changed everything. Not at first; certainly not all at once. Having it at home was expensive at first; you paid by the hour to use a telephone modem that screeched and shrieked when you tried to open a new page on the World Wide Web. It was pooh-poohed at first, but when America Online came along and made it so user-friendly that even the most technologically challenged could go online, more or less, well, that was the end of New York as its denizens would know it.

Of course, I've simplified a great deal here, but the fact is: The power of New York, at least historically for artists wishing to break through the din clamoring *me-too me-too me-too*, had stemmed from its consolidating the workings of fame and fortune into the hands of the few who were the movers and shakers in New York and Los Angeles. They held a stranglehold on distribution channels to which only bookstores and broadcasters listened and marketed. Most bookstores wouldn't touch your self-published books because trade distributors wouldn't carry them; if they did, they'd make it a big hassle for you, and you'd have to pay upfront for the offset printing of your books. If you wanted to make a film, you had to pay a truly massive fortune to the laboratory to develop the footage you'd shot. Now? You can self-publish your book, which can be carried by the major trade distributors with a matter of a few clicks online, and you can use the video camera on your smartphone and your computer to create and edit a film that can be uploaded online where potentially millions can view and share it with their friends. Film stock? Digital videotape? What's that?

Friends there tell me that New York isn't what it used to be. Of course. Each subsequent generation will hear this refrain, and they too will tell their friends the same thing. New York is a city built on hyperspeed change, sometimes way too fast until it's too late, and then everyone will mourn what's been lost. The rent situation, which is truly way out of control in comparison to my time, is such a change. People are already moaning elegies for the lost rent-stabilized apartments in Manhattan and how so many people are buying up apartments, but oh, that's nothing; just you wait. New York will still have those legendary landmarks, but its soul, usually fired by the collective hunger of so many—oh, always too many!—young artists eager to prove themselves, will be filled with ghostly echoes. Tourists will walk its streets and snap a zillion pictures, but that'll be pretty much it. The startlingly new won't always be found there. That will be what's shocking about New York.

I left Manhattan not because of my amicable breakup with my partner of fifteen years, though there was that; after my first rent-poor year in New York, I had told myself that I would *never* go through that stress again. Just not worth it to suffer it all over again; no landlord was worth my stress. No, I left because I saw the writing on the wall. New York, no matter how it may delude itself, is no longer the center of the universe it once was, at least for writers like myself. The internet is now the new temple in which reputations are forged and worshipped. Suddenly, with a bit of ingenuity, you could create video clips designed to go viral in ways unthinkable back in the late 1980s when I moved to New York, far more quickly than trying to get the attention of an agent or a publicist. Anyone can be a star, and any writer, if they're savvy enough, can get their work distributed to bookstores and online vendors quickly. Many well-written books do eventually rise up to the top, not always with major sales but with critical acknowledgment, but that's always been true before even with traditional publishing. Getting the attention of feature editors in print newspapers remains difficult as ever, but as more and more people read their news online, it's possible to spread word about your new book quickly via social media and elsewhere.

Of course, people still believe that to be a "star," you need credibility, recognition from those considered credible in the media. You need to get the stamp of approval from the kingmakers, but in an era where more people can have instant distribution worldwide, New York's kingmakers have less power to dictate who will be the next stars. New York is not the dream factory it used to be.

No less than Patti Smith, the Godmother of Punk herself, said this some years ago: "New York has closed itself off to the young and the struggling. But there are other cities. Detroit. Poughkeepsie. New York City has been taken away from you. So my advice is: Find a new city." She's unfortunately right.

Do I miss New York? Oh, God, yes, but it's not my city anymore. It is a mausoleum of my youth, my unfulfilled ambitions when I lived there for seventeen years; yet, when it tried to break my spirit over and over again, it forced me to become a better writer. I had to rethink, create faster, be willing to cut entire swaths of filler prose; imbibe more deeply the alchemic mysteries embedded in each book I'd bought at half-price at the Strand. But there are only so many seats available at the altar.

Does this mean I was a terrible writer? I don't know; I was just unlucky with connections.

Am I bitter about it all? Oh, God, no. I don't regret leaving when I did.

When I moved to New York, I wasn't thinking about becoming famous. I moved there because the city had inspired me in ways that no other place had. I moved there because I sensed that it would have much to teach me about writing, my first love; that it has, and for that I have New York to thank. Today I still write, as I always have since I was eleven years old, because my heart, my art, depends on it. Writing is what keeps me alive. I'd still write even if I knew I wouldn't make money off it; what matters is the passion, that feverish dream of telling a story so clearly, *just so*, no more or less, that one day, perhaps years after its initial publication, will spark recognition and appreciation. Am I being too optimistic? Yes, I believe so, but I know I have a voice all my own. One day its nasal timbre will ring out, a clear bell cutting through the white noise of our chaotic age, and be heard. Many writers have never lived in New York and succeeded; whether you feel encouraged wherever you are, whether you feel enabled to thrive is truly what matters. The last seventeen years here in Minneapolis have been extraordinarily kind to my output, and this is mainly because I don't have to stress too much about whether I'll have enough money to pay my next month's rent. Put another way, in my seventeen years in Minneapolis, I've had twenty-four books published, versus the five books published in my last twelve years in New York. Right now, I am indeed writing the best fiction of my life. True, I'm older and more experienced, but the pace here suits me better. I discover, evolve. I've become a better dreamer. It's more than just words.

New York, New York: Oh, I'll always love her, but my baby's become too expensive. She's become an oversized shopping mall for the haves, more so when each tenant in those preciously fewer rent-stabilized apartments expires, making way for the next in line on a very long waiting list. My baby may say that she's for the arts, what with her amazing museums and galleries and theaters, but she's no longer for the unknown artist. She's pushing him out until she herself won't matter as much, a memory that will surely become fiction of the future. Future generations will wonder how artists, at least those without trust funds, ever once survived there in the first place. She's the first love I'll always remember with a great fondness, even forgetting how high maintenance she had been when I lived with her, but I've changed too much to want her back.

CHANTS OF SILENCE

Come worship the kisses of sun and satyrs gathering around in this circle. Some of us are naked; most of us wouldn't survive the first cut of potential centerfolds for pornographic magazines. Some of us don dresses and halter bras, while our long goatees are braided; we dab our eyelids with stark glitter, and we celebrate the complete absurdity of gender expectations with our fashion felonies with prances and laughs. We are satyrs of the sun . . .

When I first heard about radical faerie gatherings, that was what I imagined would happen. I wasn't sure if I'd feel included at such an event, because it's just too hard to speechread if people are always moving their heads or arms, or if they want to chant in the flickers of a fire.

But then again, I've never felt like the type of person to join other people when they chant.

In the magazine racks in the back of Lambda Rising bookstore in Washington, DC, I came across a copy of *RFD*. I was completely taken with it, because as someone who grew up in Michigan's Upper Peninsula, a land of small towns, I found the idea of gay people *choosing* to live out in the country—as opposed to feeling the need to congregate with their own kind in large urban centers— to be quite enthralling. I'd understood that being gay meant being unconventional, so *RFD*'s unconventionality in layout and tone thrilled me to no end.

———

The first picture I saw of a radical faerie gathering was in a book—or was it a magazine, perhaps in *RFD?*—back in the mid-1980s. A small group of men, mostly strange-looking and unattractive by the A-list gay men's standards, all gaudied up, were holding hands up in the air somewhere in a sunny gasp of the woods. It was as if they were the *anti*-drag queens of drag. But their looks of exuberance were undeniable.

When I'd come out as a freshman at Gallaudet in August 1984, I had mixed feelings about the Catholic Church. The more I read up on the history of homophobia, the more I realized that I had to denounce my involvement with the church for their ongoing role in homophobia.

Becoming more aware of Deaf history, as well as learning stories that had been passed down without much of it documented, I had to question the role of religion in society. I attended masses given to the members of Dignity, a gay Catholic group, at Georgetown University. Even though it was interpreted, I came away vastly disappointed. How could any gay man attend Mass and *not* feel rage at an institution that hadn't hesitated to use its power against LGBTQ+ people? I found the whole spectacle incredulous.

I dabbled in Zen Buddhism, but being a twentysomething filled with hormones, I found it tough to sit still, so I gave up.

Two years later, I studied the history of witchcraft and paganism in the United States. I read Margot Adler's *Drawing Down the Moon: Witches, Druids, Goddess-Worshippers, and Other Pagans in America Today*, which I found to be an absolutely gripping text. I even contemplated the idea of becoming a pagan of sorts, but as a college student, I had to deal more with the reality of getting through school.

After I turned in my report on the book, I was delighted to see a pair of faeries walking up Connecticut Avenue from Dupont Circle. I'd read some about them but never saw them in person. The taller man wore dark turquoise lipstick, a necklace of ordinary stones, glittery nail polish, a reedy moustache, and a t-shirt that wondered AIN'T I A DRAG? His wispy friend sported a full beard with dabs of rouge on his cheeks, denim cut-offs, and a pair of cowboy boots.

My Deaf friend said in ASL, transliterated here in English, "These-two weird!"

"Not think s-o."

"What? Why?"

"Them force people stop expect-expect everyone look same. I-f everyone *require* look behave same year-round, same hearing people, then no room Deaf people finish."

He said nothing.

Did I try to shock with my own clothes? Only a little, as I didn't feel confident enough. It's tough enough if you're Deaf, having to educate people so that you can speechread them; many hearing people never realize the amount of effort that goes into speaking clearly enough and what a damning art speechreading truly is. So much depends on context and acoustics. Furthermore, many hearing people feel intimidated by the idea of approaching a Deaf person in the first place, so if I tried to drag up as a faerie in appearance, I'd have alienated even more people.

When I was 18 years old, I read Quentin Crisp's autobiography *The Naked Civil Servant*. I was stunned. I had never read anything like it, certainly not with that keen voice of his. I scoured pictures of him with his fedora hat, ascot, cane, and suit.

Some years later, I had dinners with him and his best friend, who was my partner. I was filled with admiration. He had stood his ground and never changed one bit even though the world around him accelerated and left him behind. I consider him the first faerie I've ever gotten to know, even though I'm sure he'd have thought the notion of men strangely dressed and prancing about and paying worship to all sorts of goddesses and gods to be "an absolute mistake," much like he'd viewed sex and music. If a faerie means being a non-heterosexual man completely independent in mode of dress and attitude among other things, Quentin certainly was one.

Years later, at a reading held at A Different Light bookstore in New York, I saw Harry Hay himself. Men-moths of all sorts, often strangely costumed without trying to hide the fact that they were still men, gathered around him. That Harry had a balding pate and stringy white long hair along with his dangling feather earrings didn't seem to faze him in the least. He was what he was; the rest of the world be damned as he sat there with his wood-carved cane. I knew of his involvement with the early gay rights organization Mattachine Society, but I hadn't quite realized that he was as equally influential in the radical faerie movement in the United States.

I try to live my life without regrets, but that I never got to say hello to him is one of them.

Then came Walt Whitman ambling into my life. I don't remember the first time I'd heard of him, but I suppose he'd been everywhere like shadows that go unnoticed until one looks down. It was in the late 1980s when I picked up a used paperback of the 1856 revision of *Leaves of Grass*. In those days, I was lonely in New York, often wondering whether anyone would want to be with a Deaf gay man who only just graduated from college. Younger readers may be surprised to learn that, in the 1980s, we gay men had to find each other the hard way: in person. Gay bookstores and bars did very brisk business back then. But out there in person, I couldn't photoshop out the reality of my hearing aids tucked behind my ears.

Once Whitman started his nonstop word-train of sensation and emotion, he deliberately sabotaged his own brakes. It was sheer madness to read him as he tried to enumerate sensation after another sensation. Each line was like a stroke in an extended masturbatory session, each quiver of body adding to the symphony of body and love in sweet tension.

One Halloween, I donned a huge black Afro wig and a hot pink dress in the privacy of the apartment I shared with my partner. He too wore drag; that year, he wanted to convey Julia Child in all her vocal idiosyncrasies. "Why, hel-*lo!*" he greeted to all our visitors.

The evening was nothing but a bunch of gay friends trying on a bewildering array of truly bad thrift-shop dresses (usually made of skin-irritating polyester), trading wigs, and adding on yet another layer of pancake makeup in the bathroom before trooping out onto the runway of our living room for another round of flashbulbs going off. By the evening's end, we were walking train wrecks.

Even though we all wore women's clothing, I still felt very much an outsider. Perhaps it was because everyone talked and laughed all at the same time, so it was tough for me to speechread or follow what people were saying. Dressing up in drag was fun, but it was all about posing for the camera more than anything else. I eventually became the chronicler of their various poses. At least I knew what went on, because I was busy directing them and angling my camera for what I hoped would be memorable shots to be enjoyed a few months later at our Christmas gathering.

Fifteen years later, in the middle of writing a sequence of poems inspired by my unrequited feelings for a gardener, the ghost of Walt Whitman appeared unbidden before me. It had been so long since I'd even thought about him. Why now? I felt his firm hand grip my shoulder as I tried not to look up into his face while focusing on the computer screen as I typed. He was all about the earth in all its moods, from lust to decay. Had I wanted to bury my heart in this rotting and rank earth too?

I ferreted out a used paperback of Gary Schmidgall's *Walt Whitman: A Gay Life*. Schmidgall explored Whitman's life from an unabashedly gay perspective, and it was then I felt a stronger kinship with the man. Flush with the revelations of lust, love, and the male body in the few years leading up to his first self-publication of *Leaves of Grass* in 1855, Whitman understood even back then that not everyone could be pigeonholed so simply. I have no doubt that if he were alive today and not afraid of what society thought of him like he had in his later years, he'd have been cavorting openly with the young men he so craved, much like the poet Allen Ginsberg had done so freely. I was disappointed to see that as Whitman grew older, he kept expanding and revising *Leaves of Grass*, so much that he drained his masterpiece of its initial exulting homoeroticism, which had been like a shock of scarlet in the mid-1850s. The deathbed edition of *Leaves of Grass* had become a mind-numbing doorstop. So many pages, and for what? Money and respectability? How could he possibly have lost his nerve? Too many of his poems were sloppy misses; his watered-down revisions, more insulting when compared with the originals. (One should track down Gary Schmidgall's *Walt Whitman: Selected Poems 1855–1892* for a good overview of Whitman's best work.) Did I truly want to grow old and play it safe like he had?

By the time I finished my gardener poems, I felt as if I'd slept with Whitman himself, having beseeched him to teach me never to forget what he'd forgotten in his quest for respectability. I awoke with my beard wet from morning loam and my fingernails black from digging up the most beautiful weeds.

Growing up as the only one deaf in a family of nine children, I often sought sanctuary in both the printed word, usually books borrowed from the public library, and the unkempt woods across the street from my house. I loved exploring the woods, and I had my own favorite places. I felt safe because the woods, just like books, never judged me. It didn't matter that I wore hearing aids or that I was starting to find myself attracted to men. In those moments, I never felt like an outsider. I was just me.

Velvet Goldmine, the Todd Haynes film about the rise and fall of a glam rock star played by Jonathan Rhys Meyers, always captures my undivided attention whenever I watch it. The film is a nonlinear love letter to what it means to be a *fan* of a pop star, at best a feverish dream. Ostensibly inspired by David Bowie's "Ziggy Stardust" character and the British glam rock scene in the early 1970s, the movie follows Christian Bale's character who, among many other things, comes out and dresses up differently. There's a terrific moment of liberation when Bale's character, hiding himself in a winter jacket, slips out of his parents' house and chucks his jacket inside the shrubbery in front of his house. In tight pants and a skimpy shirt, he hurries along the street even though it wasn't exactly warm. Then he tries to walk nonchalantly past a group of people his age who are dressed up. His look of longing to fit in with them is memorable.

I'm still at a loss why this film isn't appreciated more; heck, it's even got a killer soundtrack!

Each time I watch *Velvet Goldmine*, I'm always reminded of how faeries have had to find each other not just in appearance but also in temperament. Outsiderhood is a frame of mind that only those who live it *get* about other people, and they accept others as they are, as opposed to treating them as weirdos and novelties.

Does a man need to dress up differently in order to be a radical faerie? I should hope not, because to be *expected* to dress weirdly in order to conform with other faeries would be no better than those men who buff up and wear the right designer clothes in order to score a hot trick at the swankiest club in town. Appearances cannot be everything to life, can they?

In hindsight, I had long been a radical faerie before I joined the tribe.

MISSED CONNECTIONS

To connect with another is to feel everything.

I once loved a jaw-droppingly gorgeous man who was filled with insecurities about his body. Even though he was twenty-five pounds overweight (which didn't really show since he was very tall with a broad chest), he kept insisting: I'm too fat. Yet he had no qualms about showing off his body online. He rarely went to the gym even though he had a membership card. He had felt deeply scarred by the men who had abused him and thrown him away. He said: I'm not good at talking about my feelings, so therapists are out for me. Yet he shared a great deal about the goings-on in his life, some details of which made me cringe, via social media.

The sheer perfection of his body made me feel insecure about my own. Could I ever be desirable to a man as hot as he? Could I feel strong enough to show off my flat chest online? Could I have a relationship with someone local who lived more vicariously online than offline? No matter how I'd tried to convince him that he was indeed attractive and lovable, which his many fans affirmed each time he posted a new selfie, I had to stop hoping for love with him and settle for a platonic friendship. It would've been too frustrating to love someone who felt doomed to victimhood. Pity has never interested me.

We are so constantly judged critically and unfavorably by others that when we enter into a relationship, we want more than anything *not* to be judged. We are fully aware that we have many flaws; society makes sure that we know this central fact. Society says we shouldn't feel so insecure about ourselves, and yet it is constantly ensuring that we remain insecure about ourselves. It is no wonder that so many of us feel like damaged goods. We want more than anything to be loved.

When a man marries a radical faerie, it is a powerful statement far more than anyone may realize. It is a big fuck-you to society, whether it be gay or straight, which expects gay men to behave in a certain way. Who says they must wear matching tuxedos? Who says they must cut the wedding cake together? Who says they must follow the heteronormative American Dream? The rights that come with legalized marriage are no doubt important for many reasons, but the statement of commitment is more powerful. It gives those of us who are true misfits hope that we too can be loved *as we are*, and not just good enough for hookups.

A healthy relationship says: We are both different, so let's communicate honestly here. We are different from other people, so we shouldn't try to be like them. Let's figure out what works for *us*, and for us only. A relationship, whether it is open or closed or polyamorous or triad, is a powerful promise that love can be accepting and unconditional.

I was once in love with a handsome man who had a history of losing sexual interest the minute he'd fallen in love.

He said: I'm usually the one who leaves, but I don't want to do that to you.

He said: Okay. I'm letting you in.

He said: Let's be boyfriends; it's the right thing to do.

He wanted to work overseas, and he thought we should marry there so I could live with him. But not once as my boyfriend did he say those three words to me. He was that terrified of uttering those three words. He couldn't have missed how deeply I'd loved him. In the end, he forced me in his passive-aggressive way to break up with him. This way, if he wanted to, he could claim it was *I* who broke up with him. I felt a long bout of sadness and anger afterward, but over time, I've come to feel a vast pity for him. A man so afraid of truly *loving* the man with whom he is having sex on a regular basis is a sad and unhappy creature indeed. This will be what I remember of him long after I've forgotten his face. He is already a ghost.

It all comes down to the way our hands speak to each other. At first, our fingertips are alive with the new language of another man's body in that intoxicating rush of discovery. The contours, the suppleness, the intensity is a different country. Love is suddenly a language with new dialects you hadn't heard before. It is a joy to master such new idioms. The way we touch each other merely affirms the words floating in the air between us. Sometimes we feel as if we're getting drunk from the source of life itself when we look at each other for a long moment. It is such a glorious and astonishing feeling; one that, if we choose to remember in the darkest hours of our lives together, will sustain us when we question why anybody would want to stay together. The more a couple spends time together, the more memories they create together to be laughed about in the years ahead. Love becomes a scrapbook, scuffed-up, bruised, yet cherished.

Friends have asked me if I still miss the man I lived with for fifteen years. In the beginning, it was hard, yes, but not so much anymore. Yet there are certain things I still miss. Holding his hand while watching a movie on the giant TV screen. Going together to a party filled with literati and glitterati. Eating a scrumptious meal together in a restaurant. The hot sex we had together in our early years is a dim memory. I remember the other things a lot more. They represent a language different from the ecstatic discoveries we'd made about each other in our softly lit bedroom; they have a more concrete shape, a stronger tactile feel. This memory means we did experience this together. That memory means we did love each other. And the rest, well—it's a little painful to remember them all because it would hurt to think that we'd somehow failed each other.

It's easy to know when a man has become less interested in you. He touches you less and less, and by then, you've become a couple quite familiar, and perhaps occasionally annoyed, with each other's quirks. The two of you will turn old and flavorless like many other couples walking beside each other on the street. Sometimes these couples converse with each other; mostly not. They do their talking late at night when they turn out the lights. Speaking with slowed-down breaths at close distance, silence has become their secret language. Knowing this gives me hope. How I long to hear again that language of love with another, for it sings so tenderly in the hearts of those long accustomed to each other, and how they can't bear to be without each other!

To connect with another is to feel everything, but to stay together is to remember everything.

SEEDS OF TRUTH

As a Deaf faerie, I have been looking for a home for a long time. The heterosexual and hearing society, including my biological family, has forced bitter seeds down my throat, hoping that I would bloom forth the flowery words they wanted to hear, as in:

"Yes, I want to be able to hear just like you."

"Yes, I want to speak clearly like you."

"Yes, I think sign language is bad."

"Yes, I want to marry a woman just like you."

"Yes, I want kids."

"Yes, I want to raise them in the Catholic faith."

"Yes, I want to be ashamed and embarrassed about sex, so my kids will feel the same way."

"Yes, I want to perpetuate the cycle of shame and ignorance that surrounds sex and art with everyone I meet."

Society says honesty is always best, but society prefers that I lie. It is no wonder that so many of us faeries often feel orphaned within our own families.

Like many of us, I find that creating art—no matter what form, medium, or genre it takes—is a strong antidote to the hypocrisy and discrimination that I've experienced as a Deaf gay man. Knowing that such hypocrisy and discrimination won't disappear overnight has enabled me to create things that I hope are honest and real. Sappy Hallmark cards do not exist in my universe. Creating art in words and images is my way of saying no and saying yes to everything that is truthful and beautiful, no matter how occasionally painful the process may be.

From the seeds of a confusing childhood, I grew into an

awkward sapling, feeling constantly uprooted from one place to another. I would like one day to feel strong as an oak tree and dig my roots deep into the ground, but like the poet Rainer Maria Rilke in a letter to a young poet, I must learn to love the questions. It is hard because I feel that as an artist, I am constantly seeking answers one way or another to the big questions of my life. This is odd because I know there are no single answers, only suggestions, and yet I insist on searching.

These days, as I explore what it means to be a new faerie, I realize that the body is a big part of what we faeries are. Yes, there's definitely a spiritual aspect to all we do, but it's clear to me that celebrating the body is a huge part of it. The body that I reside in has forced me to reconsider what it means to be naked in the face of desire and intimacy. I want so much not to be ashamed of my body's many flaws, and yet I ache for lasting moments of closeness with a man. My favorite part of sex is not so much the orgasm itself but its aftermath, where we don't treat each other just like another hookup; we bask in the glow of having welcomed each other sexually and physically into ourselves. In that moment, nothing else matters.

In the heat of passion, we are allowing ourselves to be in touch with the very things that embarrass us or sound silly in hindsight. Through sex without inhibitions, we tap into the certain strength of what makes us wholly unique, illuminating that we need not be ashamed of what makes us orgasmic. It is what it is, and our bodies are what they are. Art operates the same way, except that it documents the snapshots from deep within our brains, taken at any given moment. Great art, like great sex, is always truthful, like an erection needing a little attention. It is my hope that I will one day be as proud of my own imperfect body as I am of my own art.

When I write, I aim to record truth, no matter what its flavor or emotion. There is so much truth to be found in fiction and poetry, usually more than in the so-called nonfiction side of things. Such truths can't always be neatly summarized in twenty-five words or less, as is often required of fiction. Art is truth in many disguises. The true estimation of a society is not found so much in its honesty but in the level of comfort it has with lying about such basic truths about itself. When any truth is forced out into the open, it is considered a scandal. This is probably why society gets quite upset over certain stories and artworks. Who can forget the infamous Robert Mapplethorpe photograph of a Black man's humongous penis hanging out of a business suit? You can't summarize its mythic power at all because it so swiftly punctures the balloon of lies we may've constructed to tell ourselves about race, sex, and capitalism— in so many words, power. Great art will always spear through the fortress of defenses that we've constructed around ourselves in order to lie.

Artists are the unsung bearers of truth. And LGBTQ+ folks are the unsung heroes of sex because we are the ones who demonstrate the lack of absolutes in sex. Let us plant seeds of truth everywhere we go, so that each one of us can embrace the sun and bloom more magnificently in each other's presence. Perhaps, then, I'll find a real home of my own.

A SORT OF HOMECOMING

My memories of Marquette are inevitably tangled with the darkness of early morning, the nip of winter air, and the dotted tiles that lined Northern Michigan University's soundproof audiological clinic some 160 miles away from Ironwood. For some reason, my annual hearing test was always scheduled at 9 a.m. in January, which meant my mother tiptoeing up the stairs and nudging me awake ever so softly. Down the steps I would go and put on my long johns, long-sleeved shirt, and athletic socks. After I had a bowl of cereal and my eight ounces of orange juice, I'd sit in the car with my mother and our driver, who sometimes picked up other passengers on the way, for over three hours while the sun seemed to take forever to awaken.

My hearing tests never varied: I sat in a wooden chair by myself and faced the audiologist through a double-paned window, raising my hand to any sound beeping at various frequencies into my overly tight headphones. Then came the bone conduction test, in which a round of sounds was transmitted, via a skeleton-like headphone that gripped around my head to the mass of bone behind my ear. The speech discrimination test—in which I was to repeat after my audiologist, who held a piece of paper in front of her lower face so I couldn't speechread—was the worst: "Say the word 'airplane.'" "Airplane." "Say the word 'hot dog.'" "Hot dog." And so on. I had to guess unrecognizable words.

Of course, my mother sat in the waiting room. I dreaded the moment when she was allowed into the room where my audiologist sat with her audiometer. They discussed her findings, the X's and O's leapfrogging each other on the audiogram, comparing the new one against the results from previous years. They glanced back at me and talked. It was as if I were some dirty secret that had to be dissected. Starting when I was four years old, I was sent two hours away to a foster home in Houghton. No one would realize that, even though I was taught well for a total of nine years away from Ironwood, I'd end up paying a huge emotional price for shuttling between Houghton and Ironwood for decades to come.

I didn't have the words to articulate my predicament then, but now, I can say what I felt: that even with eight siblings and two living parents, I felt like I'd already become an orphan.

During my first year in Houghton, I cherished those first few weekends home with my biological family. The visits were full of excitement; my siblings, being younger then, were happy to see me back in their midst. But the novelty soon wore off. It slowly dawned on me that my siblings were busy growing up without me during the week so that, when I did show up on weekends, I was treated as an afterthought. They were always full of chatter I couldn't follow, which didn't lessen my sneaking suspicions that I wasn't really wanted. Couldn't they just stop babbling and take turns, so I'd know where to speechread? Their communication needs were treated as more important than mine; after all, they were *hearing*. During family meals, I dutifully ate each morsel off my plate while I wondered why everyone was cracking up. No one followed up on their promises to explain later what I'd missed. (Deaf people call this the Dinner Table Syndrome. This is unfortunately true of far too many hearing families who do not sign with deaf children, and it's a major reason why many Deaf people don't interact much with their hearing families.) Each weekend, "home" made me doubt whether I belonged with these people who happened to share my last name. I sought solace from snuggling up to our furry Siberian husky.

From fifth grade to my freshman year, I stayed full-time in Ironwood. Those years attending Ironwood Catholic were the worst of my life. Some boys had designated me the runt of the class and constantly picked on me. I tried to explain to my mother what was going on. She said, "So go laugh *with* them!" It would be years before she'd finally understand the extent of what I'd endured. I was relieved to return to Houghton, because at least I wouldn't be the only deaf student in high school. By then, the deaf program had allowed the use of sign language.

Losing one's parents to death is one thing, but orphanhood is far more painful when you see that your family's love for you is conditional: If I am to earn their love and acceptance, I must be a hearing, heterosexual, married, Catholic Republican. In their book, I have failed: I'm a deaf, gay, agnostic, single man. But I've gradually realized that my hearing family has utterly failed me.

At sixteen years of age, I knew I was gay, but I hadn't told anyone. One day after school, I went to a newsstand on Shelden Avenue in Houghton. I happened to spot a copy of *The Advocate*, a biweekly LGBTQ+ newsmagazine, with one of its headlines near the bottom of the cover shouting DEAF GAYS. My heart stopped. Seeing those two words was life changing. I knew from my furtive encounters with married men that I wasn't the only gay person in the world, but for some reason, I'd thought I'd be the only *deaf* gay person.

Standing there, I suddenly had two problems. A clean-shaven college student had caught my startled look when I saw *The Advocate*. He was watching me from another aisle as he pretended to browse one mass market paperback after another. I wasn't sure how to read him. Did he want a friend, or was he looking for sex? The other problem was my age. *The Advocate*, though clearly a gay periodical, wasn't placed with the pornographic magazines in the uppermost rows, but I still worried there might be an age limit. Would the bored female salesclerk stop me from buying it? I tried to play it cool by simply picking up a copy without leafing through it at all and walking to the cashier. She rang up the sale without so much a glance up, and I quickly put it in my backpack. I was too terrified to look back at the college student, whom I never saw again and would always wonder about in the years since. Was he truly gay like me? Who was he? Was he from the Upper Peninsula too? But I didn't allow myself to dwell on such questions as I hurried alongside the highway for two miles from downtown Houghton to my foster family's house with the fire of my secret burning inside my backpack.

Later that night, in the privacy of a bathroom, I fought back tears of joy when I read about the Deaf gay community thriving in New York City. Knowing that I wasn't alone as a Deaf gay man gave me strength I didn't know I had. Knowing that my true family was waiting out there gave me the hope I didn't know I needed. So what have I learned in the years since? First, you need to believe that you are indeed worthy of love and acceptance as you are, even if your own family insists in nonverbal—and sometimes verbal—ways that you aren't. It's hard to love yourself as you are when no one tells you: *Hey, you're cool.* But, my dear reader, you are so worth the effort.

Which is why I so admire the folks who work hard to put together the annual Upper Peninsula Rainbow Pride (UP Pride). This event isn't just about visibility and awareness of the incredible diversity that comprises the LGBTQ+ community; it's about making those who don't feel loved and accepted in the UP feel welcome, as in *home.*

Pride festivals around the country have always struck me as family reunions of sorts, but the UP Pride Festival is extremely special to me. Even though I've lived in large cities since I left the UP in 1984, I'm foremost a Yooper (for UP-er), and though I'm never there enough, this homeland of tree and snow has continued to nurture me. The endless miles of forest that grace the two-lane highways veined throughout the UP are echoes of the home I've ached for all my life. It is said that trees clustered together weave roots among themselves so that, if a tree is chopped down, they can still feed the stump left behind. I still feel the roots of my old life tug at my heart from time to time.

When I return to Marquette this time, it's not to take another hearing test. The UP Pride Festival will be a homecoming. When I perform my work onstage in ASL, I will do so in honor of every LGBTQ+ Yooper who has wondered if they were really alone. My dear reader, we are never truly alone. We just have to find the right family.

OF HANDS, TENDERED

THE POWER OF GLANCES

At first, the glances from the others didn't bother me. In the 1960s, I was a little boy outfitted with a bulky hearing aid on his chest. It must've felt like a toy at first, but I am sure I didn't find the oversized earmolds to be entirely comfortable. I had been only a floating amoeba on a constant collision course with my then-six siblings. I didn't quite understand that *I* was supposed to speak, but I had sharp eyes. I tagged along like a duckling after my siblings on their adventures in the living room, around the backyard, and wherever our father took us in his station wagon.

But the second I was placed in front of my first speech therapist, I knew something was terribly wrong. No, it wasn't just the fact that I was the only one with a weird thing on my chest with beige cords snaking up to my ears. No, it wasn't just how I was expected to sit in front of a strangely smiling woman who kept pointing to pictures, trying to show me the words I had to pronounce. Wanting to please my mother, who sat next to me in an empty classroom on the second floor at Norrie School, I tried to mimic the movements on my speech therapist's lips. She insisted that I touch her throat where I could feel the nasal vibrations. Somehow, I made the vital connection between image and text and speech. I'm sure when that happened, it became a real Helen Keller moment for my mother.

It would take me many years before I could articulate what I couldn't back then. I had been used to pointing and gesturing for whatever I wanted. Even though I saw hearing people use their mouths for talking and laughing, it wasn't my style. I was more comfortable with my hands saying things I could instantly understand. I was reaching out into the ether for a spirit language waiting to be claimed. It didn't have a name, but it glittered on the periphery of my dreams. I didn't know that sign language existed, nor that I would be forbidden to use it. I didn't know it then that starting with my first speech lesson, they were training me to become an impostor.

It's quite extraordinary how a deaf child like me, having had no exposure to ASL until later in life (my parents had tried to ensure that I didn't see anyone signing whenever we were out and about), had an instinctual grasp that something was amiss. But once I was part of a deaf speech training program, a Deaf girl, who had learned to sign but was forced to speak, showed me my first ASL sign in secret: "BOTH." In a flash, my soul said *yes*.

Once I was finally permitted to sign at the age of fourteen, I realized I had to harness the power of the glances that had hounded me all my childhood. For years, I'd shriveled from hearing classmates and strangers gawking at me whenever I opened my mouth to speak. Their ignorant reactions shamed me. No one wanted to be my friend. The loneliness got so bad that I did try to commit suicide, but my overdose wasn't strong enough. I woke up, surprised and disappointed that I was still alive. I never told anyone until decades later. But once I felt at home with signing, I had to resist their withering power of staring. I learned that the best way to survive their glances was to welcome them. Allow them to gawk. Allow them to wonder what the hell I am saying with these hands of mine. Allow them to feel pity for me because I don't speak.

It wasn't just the articulation of my hands that gave me strength. It was, in my first year at Gallaudet, seeing with my own eyes that I wasn't alone as a Deaf gay man. The students, too, showed me that signing openly wasn't all that different from being openly gay. If you know anything about Deaf history, you'd know that many of us weren't allowed to sign, so we had to sign discreetly at waist-level rather than in the customary space in front of the chest. I learned to look at my friends not with shame or embarrassment but with pride. I learned to assume that everyone knew I was gay, and I lived accordingly. I soon learned that I could never win with my own hearing family, who didn't like the fact that I refused to hide being Deaf or gay. Until that moment of solidarity when I began learning ASL, I had always averted my eyes from everyone's. Sometimes I broke down in tears. But with the liberating power of ASL and the kinship with other LGBTQ+ people, I felt proud enough to stare right back. My eyes now say: I shame you because you feel entitled to look down on me. I shame you because you don't know how to sign. I shame you because you find the idea of romantic love beyond the heteronormative unacceptable. I shame you because no matter how you try to punish me with those glances, I still have these beautiful hands. I am language reclaimed for that Deaf gay boy who had needed my hands far more than a speech therapist's hand on his throat.

TOUCH

Many hearing people consider music the universal language, in that it truly connects with people in ways where all other languages fail. I disagree.

No one seems to realize that touch is the most powerful language of all. Babies respond more viscerally to touch. So do lovers. So do husbands and wives after decades of marriage. So do new friends learning about each other. The touching and affection we receive affirms our primal need to be reassured that we do indeed exist, however insignificantly, in the wider scheme of the entire universe. A lack of touch can even define how people live, often leading to tragic ends that music cannot salvage. The language of touch—or the lack of it—will often define a person's lifelong attitudes toward love, sex, and humanity, as well as child development. Clinical research on touch deprivation, in samples ranging from infants to adults, has reinforced the power of touch in infant development (babies who were massaged frequently versus babies who weren't did vastly better in their development) and adult mental health (not enough physical affection has been shown to increase stress, depression, and anxiety).

In my view, any sign language—not just ASL—is a step closer to the universal language that mankind has always hungered for. I'm not even talking about Gestuno (or Esperanto, for that matter). The language of touch is inexorably entwined with the language of hands: both are precise and physical, often demandingly so. To sign is to communicate with the entire body. It is almost as if Deaf signers are natural-born performers, as if anywhere they talk with another Deaf person becomes a stage. Even if I see Deaf strangers talking on the street, I feel as if I know their lives—not the facts, but their nuances of living—in that spellbound moment of discerning their signing: I'd know right away whether they were native signers, raised orally, and so on—things that few hearing people could catch in a single glance. The body itself is the most powerful tool that we have for changing the world, and through our bodies alone can we truly comprehend the language of touch.

There is a lot more physical affection between Deaf people when they meet. The fact that they sign openly in a hearing world attests to a simple fact: Sign—I'm thinking of the multitudes of sign languages around the world here—is a language of survival. When Deaf people were constantly shown how worthless they were, they fought back with an all-consuming desire to communicate. They didn't know language, but language from within sprung forth in their hands. That is probably why, for me, when I first began learning ASL, I had picked it up so quickly. I wanted my hands to be my emotional feelers, not my voice, which I had to think about all the time whenever I spoke. Did I pronounce the words correctly? Did I use the correct words? Did everyone understand me? With ASL, I can let go. I can dream without stopping. I can compress a five-minute deadpan spiel of English into a minute with full conveyance of emotion.

So why do Deaf people seem to take forever to leave a party, an open-captioned movie theater, or a Deaf theater production? They're starving for comprehensible communication. They can't get enough touch through their hands, and they can't ever share enough of how they were touched. They compress much more of their personal experiences, often bluntly and without shame, in a half hour than most hearing people can in a four-hour dinner party. Deaf people's craving to communicate—as if to touch language itself—is so naked that it can almost be embarrassing at times to watch.

No wonder Sign is often considered dangerous. Learning it forces you to become more aware of the signals that your own body sends out, which can be very difficult for many hearing beginners. All their lives they could take cover behind their voices and pretend; now they can't. All of a sudden, they find that they may not have as much control over their physical inflections. And the bluntness that seems so predominant in ASL—what are they going to do about *that?* They often don't want to admit that Deaf people have figured out something before they have: Life is too short to waste on a wall of meaningless words, to distort the truth, to misunderstand. Directness is a virtual prerequisite of Deaf culture. Growing up in a hearing world, I was initially shocked by this quality when I began learning ASL, but being an ASL signer for more than thirty years now, I find that I much, *much* prefer it to the obtuseness of the English language.

For those willing to take the leap and trust their bodies, ASL is highly addictive. Speech therapists know this, which is why they are so adamantly against it. To communicate from the body within is a powerful force that doctors and parents would dearly love to control, so that their own hearing world can persist as before. That's why Clayton Valli, in an ASL poem, compared ASL to weeds. No matter how hard hearing people try to choke off ASL, it still reappears like the beautiful dandelion it always has been.

I'm a happy ASL addict. This is not a drug that I'd ever give up, and I am so grateful that there is no such group as ASL Users Anonymous. Believe it or not, contrary to what you might've read, ASL is very safe. It can be consumed anywhere without harm to one's own body, and no preparation is needed: in fact, you can use it the second you see another Deaf person coming your way. I like getting high on my hands in motion because I feel in total control of my own body. In fact, it's often so contagious that Deaf strangers, meeting for the first time on a train platform, will often share in just a few minutes their most personal opinions. No doctor or speech therapist can ever hope to eradicate ASL from our bodies, because it's too far close to the bone of touch. Even if this can't always be articulated, we all somehow know that to be deprived often of touch means to die; that is why love—or the lack of it—figures so prominently in our lives. With each touch, we can feel good about ourselves and reaffirm ourselves as a people. When we unify as a people, we can survive against all odds.

AGAINST A UNIVERSAL LANGUAGE

I am totally against the idea of having one universal language. It doesn't matter if the language in question is English, ASL, or any other foreign language. The concept of being able to converse with anyone in the world using the same language is a nice fantasy, but if this does happen, we will lose more than just languages deemed unworthy and therefore driven to extinction. We will not seem as diverse as we truly are.

When I first arrived in Berlin, Germany, I did not know any German words other than *achtung* (attention) and *auf wiedersehen* (goodbye). At first this worried me, even more so when I realized how they deemphasized the use of English in store windows and elsewhere, but the more I stayed in Germany, the more I saw that I needn't have worried. I didn't have to speak English; the fact that I gesticulated what I wanted didn't bother the shopkeepers in the least. I was just another tourist who didn't know German. If I tried to gesticulate the same way here in the United States, the salesclerk would typically feel flummoxed. The more exposure that people have to a wide variety of foreign languages, especially with people from other countries, the more they are able to adapt to people who don't speak at all. This would certainly make life a lot easier for Deaf travelers.

Furthermore, the richness and diversity of languages is as essential to our diversity as a species as much as the variety of animals and flora in the Amazon rainforest is to the existence of the larger global health of our planet. We are truly interconnected, and a single language alone is not going to keep us connected. We need indigenous tongues—and hands—to remind ourselves just how unique each of us is. For instance, Switzerland requires its daily newspapers to print the same report in its three national languages! It has been said many times that each language grows its own culture and associated legends. Latin, as dead as it is now, was initially useful in our need of taxonomy, the naming and categorizing of the living things around us. Imagine how differently we might call certain plants if Latin wasn't such a huge influence, or how different our ASL signs might be if Laurent Clerc hadn't brought over his French Sign Language. As much as we desire purity in the grammar and vocabulary of our languages, the truth is that languages that survive the longest are the ones that get dirtied from time to time. That's where commingling words and useful phrases from other languages help. They are each language's badly needed transfusions of blood and culture so that in spite of the initial barrier of not understanding each other's language, we actually become closer in ways that we can't always explain. That by itself is a healthy thing. Who said that we had to explain our acts of extemporizing? If it feels right, there's probably a compelling reason, though we may not realize it until later. By then, it may've entered our language, seemingly out of thin air.

Knowing just one language means that we become very lazy when we communicate with each other. We begin to take each other for granted, which in turn can be a huge source of friction if one person feels slighted when not listened to. But with languages not our own, we either wake up or give up. In the United States, we've already given up even though Spanish is making such strides that it is becoming a *de facto* second language. On the other hand, Deaf people have not given up on their own sign languages. They've already intuited that knowing *only* the spoken and written language of their hearing counterparts is the surest road to failure in that all-too-human need to communicate and connect.

A IS FOR AMERICAN: A BOOK REVIEW

How I chanced upon Jill Lepore's book *A is for American: Letters and Other Characters in the Newly United States* (Alfred A. Knopf, 2002) is rather like how the stories of its seven characters are told in this book. Initially, when I read in Mabs Holcomb and Sharon Wood's book *Deaf Women: A Parade Through the Decades* (DawnSignPress, 1989) about the famed inventor Samuel F. B. Morse's deaf wife and that "they communicated by using Morse code on their hands," something went off in my head. Something about that story didn't strike me as right, but what? I decided to do a little research on Samuel Morse and his second wife via Google, which showed in a sample of Jill Lepore's book that when Morse was in the market for his second wife, he said to his brother that "her misfortune of not hearing, and her defective speech only excited the more my love & pity for her." It turns out that marrying a poor deaf woman was Morse's way of feeling "doubly & trebly sure" of "her sincere devoted affection." That revelation led me to read the rest of Lepore's book, which is unlike most historical nonfiction books I've read.

When the United States finally won its independence from England in 1783, the question of what makes a country a *nation* became paramount. Yes, many of the colonists spoke English, but how could we make ourselves wholly distinct from our forebears now that we had a country of our own? As language and its implications were key to that discussion during the first century of America's history, Lepore explores this question through the lives of seven men who tried to answer that nagging question: Noah Webster, William Thornton, Thomas Hopkins Gallaudet, Samuel F. B. Morse, Sequoyah, Abd al-Rahman Ibrahima, and Alexander

Graham Bell. (Three of these men—Gallaudet, Morse, and Bell—have the curious element of marrying deaf women, but according to Lepore, none of them met each other.)

Aside from these three men, why should Deaf readers care about the other four? Plenty. All of these men contributed to the larger dialogue of what it meant to be a nationalist, and how its corollary, language, should be used. Lepore explores this by starting off with Noah Webster. An extremely unpleasant man in person and in writing, Webster is still remembered for having produced the first dictionary in this country. Not only that, his spelling book sold approximately a million copies, which in turn influenced how we came to spell in the American way. He thought the idea of dropping "ou" as in "favour" versus "favor" ridiculous and resisted it in his own writing. But his thoughts and concerns on the conventional spelling system of a language, or orthography, were indeed crucial to the creation of a national identity. Before Webster, writers varied their spelling of the same word on the same page, so there was never any consistency. He felt that if spelling could be standardized, every American would be able to talk the same way.

Then along came William Thornton, whom Webster came to hate. Thornton, himself an immigrant from the Caribbean who'd won the competition to design the United States Capitol in Washington, DC, aimed to create a "universal alphabet" in order to unify all the countries in the world. But these attempts failed, partly because the concept of a universal alphabet didn't take into account the concept of cultural shadings inherent in each foreign language. Lepore's book explores the politics of the times, particularly with the sea changes happening politically in France and the subsequent fears that our fledgling country would be thrown into similar chaos. It becomes clear that the crisis of defining ourselves as *Americans*, rather than just a country of immigrants, wasn't an idle one. As a result, Webster announced plans to compile a "Dictionary of the American Language." Because he was so unpleasant to begin with, his dictionary idea got booed in practically every quarter. But he didn't give up. In order to get his dictionary published, he had to give up on his ideas of spelling reform when his printer said that they'd standardize the spelling their way.

Lepore included a chapter on Sequoyah, which seems to be

the most relevant to our ongoing history of Deaf education in a circuitous way. Sequoyah was an Indigneous American who invented a Cherokee syllabary, a set of written characters representing syllables, which became for the Cherokees far easier to master than the English that Christian missionaries had tried to teach. While I won't go into great detail here about how he came to develop his syllabary, I should mention the thoughts that flashed through my mind as I read this: Christian missionaries, and their attempts to preach the superiority of their religion to whom they considered "heathen" or "savages," could be compared to advocates of speech-only education, as some people had considered deaf people who couldn't speak to be savages, believing a lack of speech had to equal a lack of intelligence. I thought it most telling that a Cherokee, not a White man, could enable the literacy rates of his people to skyrocket to the point of being on par with their White counterparts. But was Sequoyah taken seriously? Yes, at first, but because he was a "savage," his invention was discounted. Even Noah Webster felt that, in Lepore's words, "a syllabary, according to prevailing theories, was a grossly imperfect, even savage form of writing." This is stunningly parallel to how sign language was viewed prior to the researcher William Stokoe's assertion in the 1960s that ASL was indeed a true foreign language on par with any spoken language. According to many oralists back in the day, ASL wasn't quite on the same level as English because it appeared incapable of conveying philosophical concepts. In any case, Sequoyah was more interested in retaining the Cherokee ways despite his people being constantly forced out from their homes, as White Americans stole their lands. I found this chapter particularly filled with resonance for the signing community.

This segues nicely into the oft-told story of how Thomas Hopkins Gallaudet traveled Europe in order to find the best educational methods to teach Alice Cogswell, his benefactor's deaf daughter, and met Laurent Clerc, a brilliant Deaf Frenchman whom he convinced to come to America with him in order to set up the first school for the Deaf in America. However, what's fresh here is Lepore's bigger-picture approach of what makes any language "natural," and her use of Gallaudet's assertion that sign language was truly a "natural language," one that he felt might be universal even. We now know that sign language is not universal; even Clerc mistakenly believed in this idea. Lepore does a concise job of explaining how this is not so. She quotes Gallaudet himself on English here: "Our language, so far from being [Deaf people's] mother tongue, is to them a foreign language." Clerc even wrote, "Every spoken language is necessarily a learned language" for Deaf people. Then the question of separatism versus nationalism is expounded through the Deaf community's controversy surrounding John J. Flournoy's radical idea of setting up a state run by Deaf people.

In the next chapter, Abd al-Rahman Ibrahima turns out to be a different case altogether. Originally captured in Africa, he was brought as a slave to Natchez, Mississippi, where he toiled for forty years. He had the curious luck of being recognized by a White man whom his father had saved from death while in Timbuktu; he was eventually freed. Actually Ibrahima was an Arab who had been raised to read and write in Arabic prior to his unfortunate capture. When people began to realize that he could write beautifully, they were frightened because it was felt that literate slaves had the power to incite other slaves to revolt against their masters. That Ibrahima's writing was in Arabic made him all the more mysterious, and his story made for compelling material in the newspapers. Throughout his story, the debate of returning freed slaves to Africa and the notion of a freed slave being able to read and write comes up over and over again. A Natchez newspaper editor stressed that "not a drop of negro blood runs in his veins. [Ibrahima] places the negro in a scale of being infinitely below the Moor." Gallaudet himself was so touched by Ibrahima's story that he toured with him for two months. They gave electrifying speeches on the tour, which helped raise money to free Ibrahima's wife and their nine children and grandchildren so that he and his family could return to Africa together.

Samuel Morse, a failed painter best known for making the telegraph a totally workable concept on a national—and then global—scale, has a surprisingly weak chapter in an otherwise strong book. Yes, the idea of using dots and dashes is interesting, but pushing to construe it as "universal communication" seems a bit repetitive after the book's earlier discussion on creating a universal alphabet. (Incidentally, I had found Tom Standage's book *The Victorian Internet* [Walker & Company, 1998], a concise look at not only the technological advances but also the social impact of the telegraph on the world to be far more revealing when compared to the internet today, which is probably why I'd found this particular chapter wanting.) Lepore gives a quick background on how various inventors had attempted to make the telegraph work, and how Morse was able to break through once he understood the concept of electromagnetism, and developed through his experimentation a feasible telegraph that could transmit across very long cables. The subsequent fortune that he and his business partner, Amos Kendall, had amassed from setting up a telegraph line enabled Kendall to set aside a few acres of land that later became Gallaudet University. (Oddly, Lepore used the old name of Gallaudet College even though her book appeared in 2002. And was I able to confirm elsewhere the story of how Morse communicated with his wife via Morse code on the hands? No, but his wife was apparently an excellent lipreader with flawed speech who could sign.)

Lepore's book ends with Alexander Graham Bell and his obsession with Visible Speech, an educational and visual method created by his father to enable—theoretically, anyway—anyone to reproduce vocally just about any word from any language just from reading the phonetic spelling of such words; this method was geared toward hearing students. Even though Bell's mother had a late-onset deafness and required the use of an ear trumpet for communication, it didn't seem to have occurred to his father to adapt his method for deaf students. Bell said, "My father invented a symbol, and, finally, I invented an apparatus by which the vibrations of speech could be seen, and it turned out to be a telephone." He patented it in 1877, but it now appears that Bell had lied about inventing the telephone. See Seth Shulman's *The Telephone Gambit: Chasing Alexander Graham Bell's Secret* (W. W. Norton, 2008) for the full story. Lepore describes Bell's growing obsession with educating deaf children, even pointing out that Bell did learn the two-hand fingerspelling British alphabet in order to talk with his mother and became a good signer when he moved to the United States at the age of twenty-three. I was a bit disappointed that Lepore didn't go into detail about how he began to let go of his initial feeling that sign language wasn't bad, in favor of speech only for deaf children. For those familiar with the historical war between speech and sign, those on the side of signers might be amused to learn that William Dwight Whitney, a leading authority on the structure, historical development, and relationships of languages, otherwise known as a philologist, said this in the *North American Review* about Visible Speech in 1868: "We do not see that [Bell] has notably advanced in a single particular or scientific comprehension of the processes of utterance." Lepore herself continues on page 170,

> According to Whitney, Bell's systems included symbols for sounds a human voice cannot make and lacked symbols for sounds it can. Visible Speech, Whitney remarked, "does violence to nature, both by introducing symbols for unreal acts, and by omitting to symbolize others having a real existence and importance." Whitney complained that no one who had not been taught in person by Bell himself could read Visible Speech. The symbols did not immediately and transparently communicate anything at all; they could communicate only what Bell personally might instruct a student to pronounce.

Even though Lepore doesn't make the connection between Visible Speech and Sequoyah's Cherokee syllabary implicit here, I suspect that readers intimately familiar with the history of Deaf education in America would draw similar conclusions.

The book doesn't explore in great detail Bell's obsession with eugenics, as in the quality of human breeding, or his fear that deaf people intermarrying would produce even more deaf children, but it's interesting to note that even though Bell was anti-immigration, he himself had been born in Scotland! The telephone alone imbued almost everything he said with the weight of authority even when later research has proven him wrong on many counts, particularly in his eugenicist rationale for keeping deaf people apart; otherwise, Bell would've been a footnote in the history of the American signing community. (Today it appears that ninety percent of children born to deaf people are hearing. Bell's paranoia was clearly unjustified.)

A is for American: Letters and Other Characters in the Newly United States is an illuminating slice through the prism of language, written and otherwise, and nationalism during our country's first century. Even though Jill Lepore's focus isn't necessarily on deafness per se, its big-picture debate on language and its power to corral a group toward specific ends, through the stories of seven people who had had a hand in shaping how we communicate, whether or not we can speak, is a worthy contribution to our understanding of just why language is so paramount.

FORBIDDEN FRUITS IN OUR HANDS

The worst thing that a hearing parent can do for a deaf child is to make it clear that signing is forbidden. (Happily, the belief that signing interferes with a deaf child's ability to learn how to speak has been proven erroneous.) However, it is human nature to seek out the forbidden. Intense longings can develop for such forbidden fruits. Once such a dream takes root, it's very difficult to expunge its stump even though the tree has been chopped down. The roots of want run very deep. So it was with me.

For five years in the Ironwood Catholic school system, I was the only deaf student in hearing classes. I didn't know ASL, but I was a good speechpreader with powerful body hearing aids under my shirt.

It is rather ironic that, given how speech therapists have historically demonized ASL, my best friend in those five miserable years was Mrs. Eleanor Fraites, a speech therapist. She dyed her hair a burnt orange, painted her nails red, and wore purple lipstick and loud solid colors. She carried two bulging bags—one that held her three-ring binders crammed with strategy plans for her many hearing students with speech problems, and the other boxes of Froot Loops. She motivated her students by rewarding them with a Froot Loop or two. Bribery? Perhaps, but it was apparently effective.

She was my best friend because she never talked down to me. For instance, she didn't seem fazed by my question of what the word "erotic" meant. (I was in sixth grade and had read the word somewhere.) Because she knew that I couldn't easily absorb the colloquialisms spoken around me by osmosis, she taught me idioms. It is thanks to her that I grasped phrases like "raining cats and dogs," which would've thrown me off-balance as a lipreader. *Wait a minute— why are they talking about cats and dogs now? Weren't they just talking about the weather?* Then one Monday in October, she gave me the assignment of writing a few limericks, which were five-line poems with two rhymes. The next day, my grandmother had a stroke, and she died that Saturday. On Sunday afternoon, I suddenly remembered that my speech homework was due the next day. Considering that it was nearing Halloween, I wrote about a witch who'd been tossed into a ditch. I didn't dwell on whether my poems were any good; it was just homework. And yet, as I wrote my first poem, something inside me clicked. I was eleven.

Soon after, I reveled in writing one limerick after another. Counting syllables and rewriting lines to accommodate my chosen rhymes felt magical. It wasn't long before I began playing with free verse. Mrs. Fraites knew I was writing poetry, but she didn't demand to see more after reading my first limericks, nor did I share my poems with anyone. From the way no one talked about poetry *or* deafness, I gathered that neither should exist. But they both did. The guerilla act of writing became my weapon of refuge in a hearing world that didn't know what to do with me, that sometimes even wished I didn't exist. After all, I had to slip into the darkness of my bedroom closet with a flashlight to learn the manual alphabet in secret from my brother David's *Boy Scout Handbook*.

I don't recall what Mrs. Fraites thought of my initial attempts, but I suspect her encouragement was enough to inspire me to keep trying. Either way, I remain grateful that no one told me my poetry in those days was god-awful, or I'd have given up right then and there. It was necessary to write badly for a long time before I could write a decent poem. I had to delude myself into thinking that everything I wrote was genius or I wouldn't have persisted—I had no emotional support system then; I felt orphaned within my own hearing family of eight siblings.

When I learned ASL in my first week at Gallaudet, I felt I'd finally found my true family.

———

Some hearing people have strange ideas about ASL. They apparently think that if they master the manual alphabet, they feel entitled to say, "I know sign language," even though fingerspelling is hardly the focus of ASL. Not only that, ASL is not "English on the hands," nor is it "broken English." It's far more complex than that, and I'm not even talking about the use of space! There have been numerous attempts to create a notational system for ASL (i.e., the written equivalent of ASL), but there hasn't been an overwhelming agreement by the Deaf community on any particular approach, and the notational systems folks have experimented with what might have proven too complicated to learn. Thanks to the proliferation of cameras built into our smartphones, the need for a notational system isn't as pressing now as it was back then when video cameras were too expensive for the average consumer. Today we can easily videotape ourselves signing and post it online or use a video-messaging app to send each other "video-texts."

Using ASL gloss in my work was a happy accident. ASL gloss is simply using English words and ASL idioms in the ASL sign order. Just to be clear: there is no standardized ASL gloss system at all. I don't think it's possible to convey even a fraction of all the rich nuances of an ASL sentence on paper. For instance, there are no mentions of facial expressions (i.e., emotional inflections), the location for each person (or animal) referenced in the signing space, the spatial relationships between these people, the sign dialects (e.g., Deaf people in Minnesota sign "favorite" differently than anywhere else in America), and so on. On an intuitive level, ASL makes perfect sense to me, but it may seem inscrutable to most nonsigners. ASL is incredibly complex, so the ASL gloss in my work is extremely sparse.

So how did I end up using ASL gloss in my work? It's very difficult for me to look at my work in English and then sign it in ASL at readings, so I eventually came up with my own approach. Here's what I do: I create two sets of printouts. With the first set, I leave my work in English alone and, with the second set, denote my translation in ASL gloss. I rehearse my gloss enough so that I don't have to rely too much on reading my printout, as ASL requires eye contact. The ASL interpreter will read both printouts in advance and voice the English text when I'm onstage. Once, after a reading

I gave, a hearing person asked to see my printout. I showed her my gloss. The seemingly odd bits of English on the paper fascinated her. Not long after, I began wondering about using gloss in my poetry. At a workshop sponsored by Zoeglossia, I shared a printout of a gloss-only poem (without showing the original English version). Aside from my interpreters, no one else around the table knew ASL. It was clear that hearing people needed some form of context to better appreciate the gloss, so now when I submit my ASL gloss poems, I often include the English version in a second column. After all, context is the key we usually need whenever we enter the room of a new poem. Sometimes a poem can seem so confusing at first that we need some initial guidance to intuit where to go while reading.

Poetry has saved me, which is why I continue to write it. I seek not only salve but also a voice that can cut through the din of my siblings babbling around the dinner table. My hands, however silent they seem to hearing people at first, have amplified my voice.

What about other folks who have yet to find a means to amplify their voices?

Perhaps if we were to "outlaw" poetry in the way that ASL was forbidden to Deaf children (and in some quarters, many deaf children with cochlear implants still aren't allowed to sign today), we might find ourselves with a wonderful epidemic of closeted poetry-addicts. The only cure for them would be reading even more banned books of poetry and ingesting one horse-pill metaphor after another until that closet door collapsed to reveal entire families breaking forth into the sunlight with their own poems—poems shining either with clichéd awfulness or diamond brilliance.

In other words (or perhaps, should I say "signs"?), my ASL gloss for the phrase "poems shining either with clichéd awfulness or diamond brilliance" would be: "poetry category two, point-there sign-sign same-old-same-old boring, point-over-there sign-sign shine-outward champ finish."

UNITED

A friend of mine sent me, which was originally sent to him by a friend of a friend of a friend, which is usually the case with email, an uncredited list of "deaf labels." Some of these labels might amuse you as they did me: Sound Barriers, Acoustically Traumatized, Deaf and Bright, Deafoids, White-Forelock-Hair Deaf, "What? No CC on TV!" Deaf, Sign Abled, Ear Shutters, Look-Ma-No-Hands Deaf, Hear-i-capped, Excessive-Ear-Wax Deaf, Deafniks, Vertigo Deaf, Acoustically Impaired, Soundproofed, Hearing-Aid Squealers, Deaflings, Hearing-Hardened, "You-Deaf?-Me-Too!" Deaf, Deaf Culture Vultures, Can't-Live-Without-Hearing-Aid Deaf, Hear-No-Evils, Backstabbers Club, Deaf-As-Hell, Hearing-Underdeveloped Deaf, and Baby-Cry-Test Flunkies. Certainly far more colorful than the tired and politically incorrect term "hearing impaired."

This prompted me to think of a certain Deaf person, whom I didn't know very well and had met through a former collegemate of mine. He pointed out that there was a huge need to change the labels of how we view ourselves as communities affected by deafness. He and his wife were devout ASL users, and they had two Deaf children.

I asked him what he meant.

The next five minutes blew my mind.

Those who know me know that I have been constantly frustrated by the Deaf community's stubborn insistence on separating themselves from other groups—hard of hearing, late-deafened, cochlear implantees, deaf nonsigners, and so on. It amazes me at times that the Deaf community, in its vocal insistence on equal opportunity and information accessibility, doesn't seem to comprehend the maxim: "United we stand, divided we fall." The last time I've seen this maxim in action by the d/Deaf community—with the label "d/Deaf," I include the culturally Deaf people *and* all other groups affected by hearing loss, such as the deaf oralists, the late-deafened, etc.—was at the Deaf President Now movement, which was more than three decades ago. That's too long a wait for the next steppingstone in our crusade to be heard in more ways than one.

Because of my books, many hearing people see me as a spokesperson for the d/Deaf community. I often feel uncomfortable in this role, not because I wasn't raised culturally as a Deaf person but also because it's impossible to speak for everyone. I refuse to try. I end up explaining the obvious differences between groups that exist under the umbrella of "hearing impaired" (a term hearing people seem to prefer in spite of our efforts to educate them otherwise). After a while, it does become tiring, trying to explain why d/Deaf people can't seem to get along: educational backgrounds and culture by themselves are topics too big to be reduced to soundbites (or "sightbites," in my case).

The concept that blew me away—and I can see its vast potential for social change in this country—is the label of "the ASL user community." This would deemphasize the fact that we are d/Deaf, but more importantly, as a linguistic community, in the same way that Spanish-speaking folks in this country are considered. Thus, this label would apply to *anyone* who uses ASL—hearing or Deaf signers. This would mean that people of *all* stripes can step forward and consolidate their strength in numbers: "United we stand, divided we fall." And come to think of it, most hearing folks unaware of the finer points of deafness can grasp this concept in a flash: either you sign, or you don't. Plus it saves a lot of time—how many times do I have to explain why, even though I look hard of hearing, I actually have a severe-profound hearing loss, which would make me deaf? I am not ashamed of signing. I am also not ashamed of my imperfect speech. I consider myself an ASL user.

Notice that I didn't choose to say: "I *am* an ASL user." This demonstrates the biggest loophole in the concept of "the ASL user community." I am extremely good at reception of signs, translating from ASL into English; but my expression skills are moderately good. Others may disagree with me on this, that I'm actually better than I give myself credit for, but nevertheless my point is this: Should we include those who *think* they know ASL? I'm thinking of certain deaf oralists and certified interpreters who proclaim themselves very fluent in ASL, but to my eyes, they have unfortunately a long way to go. Notice that I am not talking about the user's deafness, but rather, the *ability* to communicate in ASL.

Or should we designate those who use primarily ASL to communicate as members of the ASL user community *only*? The hard truth about being d/Deaf is the fact that whether we like it or not, we live in a hearing world. For the longest time, when I was a student at Gallaudet, I kept wishing that the whole world was d/Deaf. When I became involved with some hearing artists in the Washington, DC area, I noticed how my wish had changed: I no longer wished that the whole world was d/Deaf, but that they'd all know ASL. That is why whenever a Deaf person shares with me her wish for a completely Deaf world, I have to ask: Is it about deafness? Or is it really more about everyone signing? Nine times out of ten, they realize what they'd meant: not a Deaf world, but a world in which *everyone signs*. The tenth Deaf person is usually a hardcore radical, demanding that everyone must be DEAF at all times in order to save a culture from sure extinction, what with so many Deaf residential schools constantly considered for closing due to budget cuts, technological advances in sound amplification devices (hearing aids *and* cochlear implants), and the increased visibility in the media of successful d/Deaf people who've managed somehow to straddle both the hearing and the d/Deaf worlds in their professional and personal lives. Worse yet, these "successful" d/Deaf people don't really use ASL! Their minds are too hearing, too polluted, too bigheaded! And so on.

Among the many reasons why the d/Deaf community hasn't made as many advances in their crusade to take their rightful place at the table in the American life is their constant judging of each other to see if they are "Deaf enough." To be judged as such, when the impact of deafness in any d/Deaf person's life varies widely in terms of education, attitude, and background, is uncalled for. To work with each other, putting aside such judgments would've been the far more constructive alternative to being seen and heard; but no, we have to deal with our "hearing" minds first. When I chose *not* to worry about being considered d/Deaf enough (or not), the quality of my life improved almost overnight. I had one less thing to worry about.

Yes, I have been deaf since the age of eight months.
I endured speech therapy until I was eighteen.
I talk to myself in ASL.
I write in English.
I talk to hearing people with my voice.
I attend Deaf theater productions.
I have Deaf friends, all of whom sign.
I watch closed-captioned and subtitled films.
I read a lot of books.
I use the video relay service for phone calls.

And so on. I don't think of myself as Deaf or hearing at all; it is only when I interact with someone new that I remember my speech, gesture, hearing aids. Am I d/Deaf enough? Am I hearing enough? I don't care. Because as long as people continue to judge each other in the d/Deaf communities, not much progress is going to get made there. Labels hurt more than help. And what's wrong with assimilation? There is a great deal more to life than being d/Deaf.

I've learned that there are no cut-and-dried answers to being d/Deaf except inner honesty. Yes, I frankly want it all—I want to be included in both the d/Deaf and hearing worlds for different reasons. Knowing full well that because I chose to write and participate in the hearing world, I refuse to feel ashamed of being the way I am. I cringe at the labels "hearing impaired" and "deaf and dumb," and I correct the speaker in question. I am very patient when I explain to a hearing person that fingerspelling alone does not validate the statement "I know sign language!" I do not lie when I am asked, "Which do you prefer—speech or sign?" I respond with my voice, but my hands are the true vehicle of my emotion.

ASL users, anyone?

THE GENERAL
(OR, WHY I LOVE SILENT FILMS)

The other day I had a hearing friend over at my apartment, and he wanted to watch a movie. Being the film connoisseur, I of course had a number of movies on DVD and Blu-Ray disc (BD), which were waiting, unopened, to be watched. One of them was Buster Keaton's 1927 classic *The General*, which had been the first silent film to come out on BD in America.

My friend said that he didn't want to see it.

I asked why not.

He said that he just didn't like silent films.

I decided not to press the issue even though the film had been often included by critics in the top-twenty lists of the greatest American films ever made. Because of this, I had bought the film without seeing it first.

When my friend left, I reflected on why he didn't care for silent films. The more I thought about it, though, the more I realized why hearing people don't care for silent films. Of course, there is a lot of stilted acting, a carryover from the days of vaudeville when one had to play to the farthest back rows of the theater, but I think it's deeper than that.

I don't remember the first silent movie I ever saw, but I am sure that I felt at home with it from the first frame. There were no sound effects nor heard dialogue; it was much closer to the reality of how I live as a Deaf person. I am constantly watching people around me, decoding what they must be saying to each other. I am used to this. Hearing people are not, and therefore they aren't comfortable with having to decode what's going on in the movie if intertitles aren't provided. They are often guided by music and sound cues to feel and react; without such cues, they feel lost. What are these people saying to each other? I never worry about the "what" part; I simply watch their body language for the "how" part, how they are relating to each other. I am sometimes amazed that hearing people do not understand just how much we d/Deaf people rely on decoding their body language. Words mean nothing when their bodies tell everything. I think that is why I love silent films so much. They capture a language that requires translating without a dictionary.

So: How was *The General*? It looks great on BD, and it's as great as they say. After a slow beginning in which the setup is explained (a train engineer wants to enlist as a soldier when the Civil War breaks out), the movie turns out to have two elaborate train chases. The speed may not seem all that fast compared to our supersonic times, but suspense fills literally every frame once the train takes off to chase a stolen train. It was shocking to realize that when the film came out in 1927, it was considered a flop. It is truly remarkable that so few intertitles were used during these two set pieces. People were expecting more of a comedy, so Buster's famous stoic demeanor ("The Great Stone Face") seemed to make it less funny. It is much more than that; it is a story of a train engineer who, rejected because he couldn't be a soldier, wishes to redeem himself in the eyes of the woman he loves. Even though it is a mere seventy-eight minutes long, it is a great example of how superfluous sound can be.

If you haven't seen many silent films, may I suggest two titles to start? Go devour Louise Brooks, the girl with the "helmet hair" who inspired the iconic haircut of the Roaring Twenties, in the G.W. Pabst film *Pandora's Box*. Her charisma, stirring a potent mix of innocence and sexual allure, nearly overpowers everyone else on the screen, so much that a woman falls for her. (*Pandora's Box* has the first filmed lesbian kiss in the history of cinema.) Their acting is completely natural, so natural that you almost don't need to hear what they're saying.

But if you want to see what I think is among the most jaw-dropping performances ever recorded on film, you must see Renée Falconetti in Carl Theodor Dreyer's *The Passion of Joan of Arc*. Based on actual transcripts of the court testimonies from Joan of Arc's trial, the film, as the most expensive production at the time, broke a lot of ground. Dreyer told the actors not to use makeup. He constantly panned the actors as they interacted with each other. He angled the camera. He directed the actors not to be "stagey." He showed how judgmental the Church could be. Dreyer continued to push the look of German Expressionism even further, but in very intimate ways. And so on. But more than anything else, you cannot take your eyes off Miss Falconetti: Is Joan clinically insane, or blessed by God? You cannot make up your mind as you watch her face. (Her performance easily blows Janet Gaynor, the first actress to win an Oscar for her work that year, right out of the water.) And the looks of these clerics leering at Joan are strikingly no different from hearing kids on the school ground judging me as a deaf boy.

Again, it is not about what they are saying; it is what they are *not* saying that interests me so. Perhaps that's why hearing people find silent films to be "boring." They simply do not know how to read body language as well as we Deaf people do. After all, body language is our master key to living among hearing people.

"THE COMPLEXITY OF REAL LIFE":
AN INTERVIEW WITH NICOLAS PHILIBERT

After its American debut at the 1994 San Francisco Film Festival, Nicolas Philibert's French documentary *In the Land of the Deaf* netted the Golden Gate Award and glowing reviews that described the film as "a warm, eye-opening experience" (*New York Times*), "completely inspiring" (*Variety*), and "seductive and magical" (*Siskel & Ebert*). Most—if not all—of these reviews came from hearing critics whose exposure to deafness was probably limited to movies like *Children of a Lesser God*, *Johnny Belinda*, and *The Miracle Worker*.

We know that hearing people's views of us—the signing and culturally Deaf—can differ drastically from the way we view ourselves, so naturally I wanted to see the film for myself.

The documentary *In the Land of the Deaf* is very straightforward. It does not attempt to preach or take sides on why or how the Deaf community should be changed. This is truly admirable, because once a person studies Deaf culture and sign language, it is very difficult to stay neutral in deafness-related issues such as the cochlear implant, the use of hearing actors in Deaf roles, and so on. Most documentaries tend to be edited to present, if not prove, a particular point of view about an issue, in the same way that a book like Thomas and James Spradey's *Deaf Like Me* was written to encourage hearing parents to use sign language with their children, or Henry Kisor's *What's That Pig Outdoors?* advocates oralism over sign language.

In the Land of the Deaf differs in other ways as well. Philibert asks us—hearing audience members, especially—to look at Deaf people in a different light. Instead of stringing together scenes to tell a story from beginning to end, he asks us to observe deaf children struggling to speak; we attend a Deaf couple's wedding, and go with them as they try to find an apartment together; we watch an older Deaf man teaching French Sign Language classes. Philibert's choice of *cinema verité*—a technique of filming unrehearsed live scenes and then letting the pieces come together in the editing room—and the few pieces I'd read about him made it clear that, unlike most hearing filmmakers interested in deafness, Philibert had truly done his homework.

In 1983 Philibert enrolled in a sign language course to prepare himself for making a film that had been commissioned to teach hearing parents of Deaf children how to sign. That film did not materialize, but Philibert did write about his experiences in making *In the Land of the Deaf* in *Traffic*, a French cultural journal. (His quotes are translated from French into English, and some are paraphrased for clarity.)

> From the first day, our teacher, a profoundly deaf man who only spoke in sign, pulled a series of drawings from his satchel. They were intended to make us understand, in terms of framing, the space which was appropriate for the practice of his language. Not only would our signs require the greatest precision, but moreover, they could not be too small or too large, so as to be inscribed within a space corresponding quite exactly to that which filmmakers would call a medium tight shot. But there would also be signs that would have to be executed in close-up, and still others, even including zooms! This allusion to the language of cinema . . . affected me like an electric shock . . .
>
> While filming signers, I discovered that I couldn't expect to frame them from a wide variety of angles as one could with hearing speakers. Although sign operates in 360 degrees, in the realm of the Deaf the "voice-off" does not exist. Out of sight, communication is not possible; outside the frame, not even a hello . . . I cannot forget that day in April 1991 when, in a [schoolyard], we tried . . . to capture the spontaneous conversation of a small group of adolescents. The camera operator, camera on his shoulder, was moving along them,

panning intuitively from one to another in the hope of arriving at the right moment on the one who was expressing herself. Standing back a little, I observed the entire scene, the sound engineer walking with his [microphone] perch, attentive to the slightest sounds [the Deaf adolescents] allowed to escape, the camera operator making his best effort, the girls chatting . . . Suddenly, I understood that the vague sounds they emitted while signing, these hoots, those little cries, the tapping of fingers, the rustle of their clothes, were not distinct enough for the camera operator to follow their movements by ear as if he were the middle of a group of hearing persons. Not being able either to hear this silent conversation or see the entire group through the camera, he worked blindly, without ever knowing where the next answer was going to come from. So I stood next to him, holding him by the shoulders, and I . . . guided his movements, at least having the advantage of being able to look in all directions. The results were just as [bad because] I couldn't anticipate who was going to sign next; it never failed that she had started to sign by the time the camera reached her. A few fractions of a second late on our "characters," we . . . missed the beginning of each sentence, even when we did not miss the whole thing completely. The conversation was much too fast.

So we decided . . . to enlarge the frame. At least the whole group would be under control. We moved back a few steps. Although one of them had her back to us, and two or three others were in profile, I hoped to be able [to figure out their dialogue], thanks to the answers which were most legible . . . [As it turned out, I had to ask] the particpants to see the sequence, I hired a professional interpreter, and I ran the scene on the editing table a hundred times, but the sequence was unreadable.

The idea of a silent film . . . was thrown away from the start. It was necessary that a film about the deaf be a sound film [to emphasize] that the world of the Deaf, contrary to what is believed, is not pure silence. I discovered that it was best to avoid any and all sound processing or artifice which would distract from the signs . . . and keep oneself to simplicity and transparency of direct sound. In other words, the hearing viewers should soon forget that they are hearing sounds while watching the film.

While subtitling the film, I realized that subtitles could not always appear simultaneously with signs themselves, for both could not be read at the same time. I decided that paced slightly ahead of the signs, the subtitles would permit the viewer to identify some of [the signs], to "recognize" after the fact . . . [It became] a game of guessing the meaning of the signs before getting the translation.

When I learned that Nicolas Philibert would be in the States briefly to accept the National Council on Communicative Disorders' Stephanie Beacham Award in Washington, DC for his work on *In the Land of the Deaf*, I inteviewed him by fax at International Film Circuit in New York City, the U.S. distributor of his film.

Have you ever had Deaf people object to the fact that you—a hearing filmmaker—have made this documentary about them?

No, I have never had a deaf viewer object because I've never tried to pretend that I could have a deaf person's point of view. All the deaf viewers have understood that. For sure, a deaf person would have made a different film.

Do you feel that because you were hearing, it took you a long time to find the "right" people to appear in the film?

From the very beginning, I worked with deaf people and quickly we became good friends. They advised me and helped me network in the deaf community. But, at the same time, they did not try to impose their point of view on me. They respected all my choices because the film is clearly my point of view. I wanted to show the complexity of real life, and so I chose people of different ages and social conditions, deaf of deaf parents and deaf of hearing parents, and the oral educational system which is unfortunately still so dominant in France today. I wanted to show the difficult conditions into which the deaf are thrust—how difficult it is to be a deaf person in the world of the hearing.

Did you have to rehearse any of the participants prior to filming?

All the scenes were shot live and unrehearsed—with the agreement of the people being filmed—except the interviews.

It's clear that you wanted to make the film accessible to the deaf, yet when I watched it, I noticed that most of the sounds generated in speech therapy lessons or in the song that hearing children sang in the beginning of the film were not subtitled. Because I don't know Frernch, I couldn't tell if the child was practicing a vowel or a word. Why wasn't all of that subtitled?

When the children sing, they are too far away from the microphone, so we cannot understand the words they are singing. That is not subtitled. When they are in the classroom, almost everything is subitled. Whenever you add subtitles, it is necessary to condense. In the same way, when people are signing in the film, I could not translate every sign. I had to condense for reasons of space and time.

In the wedding scene between a Deaf couple, I noticed that the minister was hearing. I was very surprised because I expected to see a Deaf minister involved in such a ceremony. In France, aren't Deaf people encouraged to go into the ministry to help other Deaf people?

What you have to know is that the situation for the deaf in Europe is probably much more difficult than it is in the United States. In Europe, deaf people are still considered "those poor handicapped," and we don't give them access to the education they need to become [holders of] professional jobs—like a minister or a teacher or an engineer. They are kept doing manuals sorts of labor, even if their intellectual capacity should allow them to do more. So there are no deaf ministers in France at this time.

During the wedding, they didn't even have an interpreter, and this was disastrous for the couple. In all of France, there are no more than fifty sign language interpreters. It's a catastrophe. I kept this scene in the film because it is meant to underline this very problem. The scene involving the deaf couple's apartment search also shows the everyday difficulties of deaf people living amidst hearing people. Maybe the scene also shows how hearing people are lost the first time they find themselves face-to-face with a deaf person. For most hearing viewers, the rental agent looks more "handicapped" than the couple and their friend.

What is the most important thing you've learned from the making of this film?

I've discovered the richness of Deaf culture. And working with deaf people for the film, I was able to develop my own visual acuity.

IMPOSITIONS:
ON *CHILDREN OF A LESSER GOD*

In October 1986, when I first saw the movie *Children of a Lesser God*, I wept when it was over. I had never seen a major Deaf character played by a Deaf person up there on a big screen, and I loved it. Both my Deaf lover at the time and I had been overwhelmed by seeing so many of us up there on the big wide screen in the packed theater; it felt as if some of us Deaf people had finally arrived as legitimate movie *stars*.

The film opens with rain and a darkness, where we catch wind chimes and a pair of lace curtains flickering and tinkling loudly in the open window frame. Then the camera pans slowly downward, where we find a beautiful woman sleeping, completely oblivious to the sounds around her. This is Sarah Norman, played by Marlee Matlin.

The image segues into a morning boat ride to the island where James Leeds, played by William Hurt, is due for a job interview to teach speech therapy at a Deaf school. The visual metaphor between the island and the Deaf world is quite clear: isolated from the hearing world, therefore backward and in need of missionaries. In fact, water—and mirrors—play symbolic roles throughout the film.

The first time we see the school, it looks like an overgrown home. These schools feel that way for many Deaf people, for when they have hearing parents who either feel inadequate with their signing abilities or simply wish their Deaf child didn't have to be around, Deaf students often find a truer home at school, where Deaf children find others of their kind in the same situation.

Once inside the school, James hears the bell ring and we catch lights nearby flashing at the same time. (Deaf people often rely on lights flashing to indicate whether the buzzer is being pressed, the phone is ringing, or the baby is crying in the next room.) Enter James into the office of Dr. Curtis Franklin, played by Philip Bosco. Franklin's back is turned to James as he pores over James's résumé and comments on how strong James's background is. It is not until a few lines later that we finally see Franklin's face. This is almost shocking—yet appropriate—that a hearing person running a Deaf school would communicate with James who—if speech therapy is to be James's forte—is supposed to be Deaf-sensitive. Throughout the movie Franklin represents, however ineffectually, the paternalism that seems to afflict hearing principals, superintendents, and "experts" who administrate Deaf residential schools.

Next we see a slow pan of James's new students, each dressed quite differently from each other. First, we meet Lydia, played by Allison Gompf; Cheryl, played by Georgia Ann Cline; Tony, played by Frank Carter Jr.; Danny, played by William D. Byrd; and Johnny, played by John F. Cleary.

In an earlier time, when I needed someone up there with whom I could identify, I would've identified with Johnny. He sat there with his books and looked totally uncool with his plain clothes; I would've admired his complete refusal to cooperate with his new teacher. But I was too gutless to do what he'd done: He refused to speak *or* sign, even to the very end of the film. My desire to be loved by everyone I knew was much too strong.

The fact that this movie was made chiefly with hearing audiences in mind—apparently without a thought to Deaf audience members—becomes even more obvious when the camera cuts to the students' reactions to James when he sits behind the desk without saying a word and tips over from his chair for no apparent reason. Then as James gets up, the camera cuts back to the students *while* he introduces himself. Combined with the fact that his introduction is a voiceover, even the best deaf lipreader in the world could not possibly follow this scene uncaptioned.

———

After that first class, James saunters down into the cafeteria. Standing in line for his food, he suddenly hears a loud crash of dishes in the kitchen and leans over to watch Sarah Norman, the school janitor. He slowly voices Sarah's outburst of anger at someone we do not see. This doesn't make realistic sense: he is clearly speaking for himself (or more likely, for those who don't know ASL), and in a *public* place.

James's excuse for voicing Sarah's signs may have worked on the stage (to include audience members unfamiliar with ASL), but each scene in which James and Sarah are alone doesn't work on film. The chemistry is impossibly forced. When a hearing person and a Deaf person are alone together signing, there is no need for voicing unless James, stepping out of character, is acknowledging the hearing audience's need to know what Sarah is saying. In other words, he is unnecessarily talking to himself.

Not only that, James's voicing for Sarah is surprisingly flat throughout the film, which seldom conveys the emotional inflections of Sarah's lines. Although James is technically not an interpreter, he would've known from his studies in the field of Deaf education that interpreters are trained not only to convey what is being said but also to modulate their voices in accordance with their client's signing. In other words, a person's angry signs should be voiced as such.

Subtitles would've been more appropriate, emphasizing the fact that ASL is a true foreign language, not as pretty gestures created to illustrate English in visual terms; however, this may prove to be too much visual overload for those unused to captions. Voiceovers for Sarah's lines would've certainly allowed more dignity to be given to Sarah's character rather than to be transmuted through James's interpretations (excuse the pun) of the events he undergoes in trying to understand the true essence of her, and ultimately, himself.

There are two more occurrences of interest in the cafeteria: one obvious, the other not. The obvious event is Sarah storming off to sit by herself at a table a distance away from James. While this is one of the more compelling characters created for a Deaf performer,

Sarah becomes yet another cinematic progenitor of an illustrious lineage that proclaims symbolically: THE DEAF PERSON IS ISOLATED.

Then two of Sarah's friends join her at the table, and she launches into an untranslated explanation of what's happened in the kitchen. We never see these "friends" again for the rest of the film—in fact, we never see even the slightest indication of Sarah's friendships with other people. With few exceptions, most hearing filmmakers apparently find the reality of Deaf people with positive and healthy friendships with others of their own kind hard to swallow because— hey, let's face it, there's more dramatic juice in isolating Sarah than showing her with friends who'd help her see that James is yet another "hearing asshole." This is very puzzling, because most Deaf people in my acquaintance strike me as much more sociable creatures than most hearing people. Deaf people inherently know that it's always a joy to converse in the way most comfortable to them.

The other occurrence is not as obvious. Franklin summons James to his table and introduces him to Orin Dennis, a math teacher played by Bob Hiltermann, and Mary Lee Ochs, Dennis's former teacher played by E. Katherine Kerr. Aside from not using Phyllis Frelich in the film, this is by far the most surprising change in *Children of a Lesser God*'s leap from stage to screen: Orin Dennis, once a militant troublemaker seeking to make a truly valid point about how hearing people have oppressed Deaf people they proclaim to serve in his attempt to bring about an employment discrimination lawsuit against the school, has become like *them*, the very people he'd once denounced in the stage play. The storm around Sarah is suddenly watered down to: Will she and James get together?

The images of water that permeate the film soon accumulate to the flooding point to indicate that water is Sarah's world. James walks near the water, looks at it from afar, and hungers to be part of her world. When it rains, James always seems to be thinking of her. We also learn that Sarah swims nude in the school's swimming pool, appropriately enough. There is no music during these sequences; this makes sense because one cannot hear underwater. Halfway through the film, when James later falls deliberately after Sarah into the swimming pool after his admission that he's in love with her, he is literally plunging into her world. But because music is considered the most universal language of all, the uses of both music and silence in this film are unfortunately clichéd.

Alone with Lydia in the classroom, James plays a record of "The Boomerang Song" and teaches her to feel the bass vibrations from atop the speaker. Lydia seems somehow completely unaware of a fundamental fact that most Deaf people are aware of—whether they want to be or not—and that is, Deaf people can *see* that when music comes on, people move and dance to a certain rhythm. From their point of view, dancing is visual, and the connection to the beat is easily made. The Deaf world is not entirely without music; a lot of Deaf people with varying degrees of hearing loss enjoy music in their own ways. I once met a Deaf man who could mimic exactly the posture and facial expressions of most any opera singer you could name, and he never once used his voice. The physical effort that goes into singing and speaking seems quite redundant when it is so much easier to let go with one's hands.

I am therefore bothered by James's attempts throughout the film to teach Lydia the joys of being "hearing" through music, and this is emblematic of James's character throughout the movie. He wants his students to speak, he wants them to enjoy music, and he wants Sarah to speak as well. Like so many others, I anticipate the day when Deaf students are not expected to be like hearing people but more like themselves: the more Deaf one becomes, the more hearing one becomes.

After Franklin convinces his employee Sarah (don't ask me how this was done, what with his clearly paternalistic attitude and inept signing skills) to spend only one hour with James in the classroom, Sarah walks off by herself with an adamant refusal to look directly at James or even to wait for the customary facial cue to begin communicating. When a Deaf person looks away, one walks up to that person and taps the Deaf person's shoulder to resume the conversation. Otherwise, the Deaf person should be left alone. As we will see throughout the film, this interaction is only one of the many examples revealing a similar lack of Deaf-sensitive understanding.

Being hearing, James reacts by refusing to accept Sarah's coldness as she had refused James's warmth. Much to her credit, Sarah refuses to respond to James's lack of signing; most Deaf people are offended when a hearing person clearly in the business of helping the Deaf community does not use signs with them. The willingness to learn sign language is the one prerogative to being involved with the Deaf.

On their first date in an Italian restaurant, James quickly learns that Sarah is unfamiliar with the assumptions that go with dining: Would you like some wine? Which entree on the menu is especially good? There is a lovely moment in which James tries not to show his frustration in explaining what veal piccata is in front of the waiter. This scene means a few things: She has not been taken out to a decent restaurant, she has not been exposed to the variety of dishes available in restaurants, and she inherently sees those restaurants as "hearing," where hearing people can show off their knowledge by ordering dishes she knows nothing about.

After they sip their wine, Sarah suddenly says, "Let's dance." She pulls the reluctant James onto the dance floor, and it is not long before she falls deeper into herself, closing her eyes and moving to an inner rhythm independently of the song and of the dancers around. I understand all that, but with her eyes closed? A Deaf person dancing in a crowd has to look out for other dancers unaware of her deafness. Poetic perhaps, but highly unrealistic.

It becomes gradually clearer that as much as James is the main character, he is merely an *observer*. He sees Sarah dancing off by herself, and he slowly backs away to watch her and the others watching her. There is a look of both embarrassment and pride on James's face, a wonderful moment of ambivalence.

At evening's end, James drops Sarah off with her giving a fleeting glance back at him just before she enters her house.

Presumably the next day, James discovers from Sarah herself just how these hearing boys in her past had been friends with her sister Ruth. She describes how they would proceed to fuck her, often without any preliminaries. It is a moving monologue, and the aesthetic power of this scene is definitely heightened for the hearing viewer unfamiliar with ASL but ruined for the Deaf viewer when Sarah turns to the window and delivers her clincher on how the hearing boys would … without looking at James. (Again, it is strongly implied that Sarah has no friends of her own, even though she works at a school where Deaf students are taught: THE DEAF PERSON IS ISOLATED.)

This scene is simply not credible. Deaf people require constant eye contact to make sure they are being seen and understood every step of the way, even more so if the interchange involves something as personal and specific as a bitterness against the hearing world. Deaf people are experts on how much misunderstanding goes on in our world, and they seldom hesitate to let you know if they've lost you while you're talking to them.

Curious about Sarah's history, James takes off for the city (unnamed, as the film was made in Canada) for a talk with her mother, played by Piper Laurie. He learns from her that mother and daughter have not seen each other for the last eight years. In the living room, Ms. Norman folds her hands and sits rigidly in her chair as she says, "We don't communicate very well." The ironic rigidity of her body language would certainly put any Deaf person off, for Deaf people must rely heavily on visual cues to respond appropriately.

James prods her on the matter of speech: Did she ever try to speak?

"Yes," Ms. Norman says. "She looked awful, she sounded awful." She explains how Sarah's sister Ruth would introduce various hearing boys to her, and how they'd treated her decently, as if she were "perfectly normal." Every parent with a child who is obviously different wants nothing more than to see that child accepted by others without being taunted. Mrs. Norman has clearly seen what she wishes to see of the situation while shutting out the obvious implication of so many hearing boys meeting and hanging around Sarah. Ms. Norman's use of the word *normal*, equating it with being like a "hearing" person, simply means that she is still unaware of Sarah's culturally Deaf side.

In my younger days, I never questioned the word *normal* when I did not think of myself as a culturally Deaf person, but rather as a person with a hearing problem. No one I knew ever used the terms *deaf* or *hearing* with me; as far as I could tell, *normal* meant *hearing*. But I've come to see *normal*—not only the word but also the concept—as a major obstacle in humanity's hope for unification as one people, instead of the current clot of nations and their conflicting religions, histories, and philosophies. As long as we continue to judge others as "could've-been-perfectly-normal" or "not one of us," we cannot hope to unify.

Sarah and James's next date takes place in a repertory movie theater showing Billy Wilder's *Some Like It Hot.* She watches the movie with occasional glances at James's clumsy interpretations of the dialogue, and the scene ends—inspired by Marilyn Monroe seducing the man she wants on the screen—with Sarah and James feeling the heat between the two of them. They go home and make passionate love.

If we are to believe that the movie takes place in the mid-eighties, why didn't Sarah tell James that she'd prefer to watch a foreign subtitled film or at least a closed-captioned video on his VCR? By 1985, when *Children of a Lesser God* was shot, the availability of closed-captioned videos was already on a meteoric rise, thanks to the National Captioning Institute's introduction of a more affordable decoder.

Next, we see James playing a game of basketball with a bunch of Deaf boys. James successfully blocks an attempt to score and catches William, played by John Limnidis, signing ASSHOLE.

Seeing this as an opportunity, he stops and tells William to say the word *asshole* more clearly. William pronounces the word correctly, and James nods; William laughs as if this James—a *speech therapist* with terrible signing skills playing on *their* turf—is indeed cool. As the movie progresses, William becomes something of a running joke: Each time we hear him speak, it is always some four-letter word at a loud volume, and often at inappropriate times. This running gag becomes quite offensive in the context of how Deaf characters are often used as a novelty in films. They are just a joke, just like how hearing people want to learn dirty signs without caring about Deaf culture and history; no respect, really.

———

James and Sarah have a conversation out on the dock, and Sarah tells him that she knows what the waves sound like. She demonstrates, combining the sign INSPIRATION with the gesture of waves sweeping upward on her body. The ASL translation answers what many hearing people have asked me over the years: Do Deaf people know what anything sounds like?

Hearing people naturally think in terms of sound; d/Deaf people think in terms of *sensation* through their other senses. Put another way, David Wright, a British deaf oralist poet, has said, "the world in which I live seldom *appears* silent . . . silence is not absence of sound but of movement."

This feeling of elation sours in the next scene in James's house. When James explains that he wants to work with her to speak, Sarah turns away. He suddenly grabs her hands and says to her, then to himself, "You are beautiful—what am I saying?" Hurt, she looks away.

Finally, he promises her that he will never force her to speak ever again.

The time for the school's Thanksgiving show arrives. As a small group of children, dressed as apples and pumpkins as part of the four basic food groups, bow to their parents' applause, I couldn't figure out what was wrong.

Then I noticed their huge costumes: If the children were actually Deaf signers, accommodations would have been made to allow them to talk with each other. But then again, if they were enrolled in a speech therapy program, they shouldn't have been at a school where other students signed.

Nevertheless, James cues his own students, now dubbed The No-Tones (a hearing pun if there ever was one), to begin signing their rendition of "The Boomerang Song." Halfway through the song, Sarah enters the auditorium from the side. She does not nod to anyone—again, she seems to be a pariah at the school—as she passes through the crowd of bobbing heads to a door opposite James.

He nods, "What the hey."

She glances at the parents enjoying themselves and feels uncomfortable. She of course disappears amidst the enthusiastic applause.

In their next conversation, Sarah confesses to James, "Don't hate me for not learning to speak."

James nods, accepts.

Before they go out for a round of poker at Dr. Franklin's house, we learn that Sarah has never played the game before and has just read up on how to play poker out of a book. James tells her how beautiful she truly is, and they leave. It's a night out with their boss, after all.

Around Franklin's dining room table, everyone seems amazed by Sarah's deftness with the cards. She demonstrates that she can play a mean game of One-Eyed Jacks, and by the end of the evening, she has earned a small booty of cash.

Back in James's house, they make love. With Sarah on top, James suddenly signs and speaks to her, "Say my name ... Say my name!" Sarah, still in motion, looks at him and gets off him: He has broken his promise.

The scene ends with apologies.

Then, we see James's students on an ensuing night sitting in front of his TV and eating chips while watching an action film with its volume turned way up. Sarah is in the kitchen, trying to boil some water. The phone rings, and James is the only one who could hear it—barely—above the din. As indicated throughout the film, the school is often *the* home for many Deaf children, in that the school provides the communicative family that the Deaf children often never had with their own biological families, which is perhaps why many hearing parents feel uncomfortable in Deaf schools.

The volume of the TV is suddenly shut off as James is about to answer the phone: The film on TV has just ended. (Was it closed-captioned? Probably not—being hearing, James certainly didn't need a decoder.) The students troop out, and James picks up the phone.

He learns that Orin's interpreter is calling to invite both of them to a small party on Friday night for Marian Loesser, a Deaf economist from Washington, DC. James interprets all this; delighted, Sarah accepts Orin's invitation and James relays her answer.

The fact that Sarah lives with James and yet has neither a telephone light flasher nor a TTY seems totally out of character for Sarah, who's supposed to be fiercely independent. She clearly wants to depend completely on James, a hearing man she doesn't know all *that* well, or she would've have taken care of such details without thinking, just like how most Deaf people do when they move to a new place.

At Orin's party for Marian Loesser, Sarah proudly informs James that Marian earned her two PhDs without having to speak. Yet, later at the party, Sarah sits on the sofa, watching Marian morosely. Ever the observer, James watches her.

When Sarah and James get home, James inquires after her mood.

She tells him that she feels so idiotic, and that because he is hearing, he wants to "take charge and control" her.

James is of course pissed off by the accusation, and finally puts her down with, "Well, who the hell are you?"

Sarah returns with a look, unable to answer the question.

James shrugs. "Right."

But almost just as suddenly, Sarah returns with, "Let's make out." James is surprised but he is unable to resist her sexual power. After they are done, she gets up and says, "No one is going to speak for me… Everyone told me what to think," and so on, though softening Sarah's final monologue in the stage play. She has finally articulated her own needs in her own words. And with that, she disappears into the night.

While James drives out in the rain, trying to find Sarah, she somehow appears on her mother's doorstep. Ms. Norman is surprised to see her after eight years but takes her in without asking her why.

The next morning in the living room, Sarah accuses her, "You never helped."

Ms. Norman confesses to Sarah that she had to enroll Sarah in that school because "I didn't know how to take care of you." (The irony here is that the school—as for many Deaf people who live and work at such schools—had become her family in heart if not in blood.)

But Sarah eggs her on: "You hated me."

We learn that Sarah's father left because he hated her deafness, and that Mrs. Norman grew to hate her own daughter because of that. "Please forgive me," Ms. Norman says.

The telephone rings. Ms. Norman asks, "What do I say?"

Sarah gestures, *I'm not here.*

The call is, of course, from James.

This is by far the most moving scene in the entire film, and it is to Piper Laurie's credit that she was able to convey a genuine willingness to conspire with a daughter who speaks in a language that's not always easy to understand.

The emotional payoff of seeing Sarah swimming in the nude in the school pool throughout the film reaches its crescendo with a naked James underwater, trying to experience what it is like to be in Sarah's world. This scene doesn't work because, again, *true* deafness is not about being unable to hear, but about being unable to communicate in a comfortable mode. James has *already* experienced true deafness by trying to sign and speak at the same time to Sarah: Clarity in communication can never be compromised.

Sarah's sojourn in the city by becoming a manicurist and saving money to go to college is strangely ineffectual for the wrong reason: We do not see her hunting down other Deaf people in the city; there must be some if the school is nearby (although we are given no idea of *how* nearby). So it almost comes as a joke when she finally confesses to her own mother: "I'm lonely." THE DEAF PERSON IS ISOLATED: Ba-*ding!*

On spring prom night at the school, James enters the auditorium, finds the music a *trifle* too loud, and greets some people he knows. Then he stands, seeming a little despondent.

Suddenly, a face appears out of the crowd: *her*.

He is shocked, naturally.

Presently, they are near a bench outside the school. A moment of awkwardness passes between them, but the electricity that charged their passion for each other is still transparent. What's there to say after so many months?

As the music rises in the background, Sarah confesses, "I don't want to be without you either."

He returns with, "Do you think we can find a place where we can meet not in silence and not in sound?" (I'm truly trying my best not to roll my eyes here.)

A heart-felt hug or something without speech or sign would've sealed the entire story, even with all its flaws, into a package with a beginning and an end.

But what follows is tacky—just plain tacky.

Untranslated over stirring music, Sarah signs, I LOVE YOU.

James responds in kind.

It is exactly the kind of thing many unfamiliar hearing viewers think of sign language: beautiful for the things we care most to say. As many of us Deaf people use ASL in our day-to-day lives, it is really just another language. (Most linguists will tell you they're constantly intrigued by ASL.)

James and Sarah make the sign for "to connect, to join," and with that the image of them enjoined (presumably in peace) fades to black. *Awwww.*

The lighting used by the filmmakers in quite a few scenes reveals some erroneous assumptions made about Deaf people's communication needs. In some of the domestic scenes, Sarah and James are romantically but heavily underlit by Deaf people's standards. Put another way, it is much more romantic for Deaf people to be able to understand each other in a brightly lit room than to guess each other's responses in a badly lit room.

Combine that with the fact that Sarah does not use much facial expression while signing. This flies in the face of ASL conventions:

Just as hearing people intone certain words with certain inflections to convey information, so do Deaf people use their faces with certain signs to convey information, often adverbially or adjectively. Apparently, Randa Haines, the director, felt that Matlin seemed much *too* expressive, therefore overacting (while it is quite normal for Deaf people to be facially very expressive). Or perhaps it was merely a reflection of Matlin's acting style. Because of this, I discovered that I couldn't always follow the "enunciation" of her signs. It could be due to the fact that her first language was not ASL; or that she did not feel entirely comfortable with the translation; one could say that Hurt did not. Matlin learned to speak and write English, then she learned signs as English-based signs, rather than as part of a language totally different from the syntax of English; she was presumably then exposed to ASL through interaction with the Deaf community in her hometown Chicago as well as working as a stage actress with ASL translations of English-written plays. Most Deaf people can tell right away whether a signer is a native user of ASL or not, a signer with a strong oralist background, and so on. Most of these nuances usually seem indistinguishable to hearing people, but after a time in the Deaf community, they, too, learn to catch the differences.

The placement of Hurt's body while he signs within the composition of most shots is almost contradictory. Why is it that in some scenes, his signs are cut off at the bottom of the frame, but not in others? It is quite clear that to reproduce signs faithfully on film, one basic convention of photographing people will have to be violated; that is, signers should be filmed from the waist up, not from the chest up. It is easy to film hearing people, because most of the communication is projected from the throat upward; but Deaf people signing must be filmed from the waist upward. Of course, this creates a certain, perhaps undesired, distance between Deaf performers and hearing audiences unfamiliar with Deaf culture. But again, for Deaf people, clarity of communication is far more important than the sheer aesthetics of cinematography. There are quite a few annoying shots in which Hurt's massive shoulder blocks Matlin's signing, which could easily have been rectified by filming their conversations in three-quarter profile. Yet, much to the credit of the cinematographer John Seale, who later won an Oscar for his work on *The English Patient*, there are no unwarranted shadows of signs on the signer's chest. (That is a considerable achievement, because I have encountered that problem myself while lighting Deaf performers for taping preliminary run-throughs of my stage plays. Apparently, Seale lit them from every conceivable angle with lots of soft light.)

All this means that Deaf performers will have to work far more closely with the cinematographer than most hearing actors, not only to look good but also to be clear and accessible to Deaf viewers.

Like most stage plays adapted for the big screen, Mark Medoff's play upon which this film was based is strikingly different in tone: James Leeds, a speech therapist with an impeccable work and academic record, is hired at a nameless school of the Deaf where he meets Sarah Norman, a twenty-six-year-old beautiful Deaf woman, who is clearly intelligent yet refuses to look beyond a life of being a janitor at her alma mater. He feels compelled by her refusal to use her voice, and somehow in his mission to convince her that speech is crucial to being part of the larger—albeit, hearing—world, they fall in love and get married by the end of the first act. The second act explores the circumstances in which Orin, a hard of hearing Deaf militant, tries to sue his school for not hiring enough Deaf people in the first place and not having enough of them in the more influential positions in the second place. The second act, which ultimately proves even more gripping due to its emotional wrangling over the politics to which the Deaf community have long grown accustomed, finds Sarah trying not to question her own status as a Deaf person, now that she is married to a hearing person—and a speech therapist at that.

Throughout the entire play, the passionate politics that have long divided the Deaf community over the past century are represented by four characters: Orin Dennis, a hard of hearing Deaf militant activist; James Leeds, the hearing speech therapist who is interested in the Deaf community and is "helping" them "improve"; his student Lydia, who is more attracted to the hearing world than to the Deaf world, and who is therefore docile and willing to please; and of course, Sarah Norman, who is clearly intelligent but defiantly refuses to "advance" herself in the eyes of the hearing world, a choice which has given her much pain. At the end of the play, Sarah decides that James—or any hearing person for that matter—is incapable of truly understanding not the fact that she cannot hear, but that she wants the dignity of being nothing less than a culturally Deaf person.

It does not help that the politics of the play are so diffused in the film treatment that the story is reduced to whether James and Sarah will ever get back together, but it is not even clear on what—or whose—terms: Most Deaf people would not feel comfortable with someone like Sarah becoming involved with a speech therapist; speech therapists and audiologists are often perceived as evil perpetuators of the hearing world's oppression. Sarah's romance with James would be viewed by her peers as a major betrayal of Deaf cultural values. If James wants to continue with Sarah, he will have to stop using his voice and use ASL to be included among her friends.

In this context, when Sarah tells James that they cannot remain together, the ending for the stage play had made—and still does make—perfect sense. The movie apparently set out with a different agenda in mind.

It is fairly unfortunate that *Children of a Lesser God* was so widely acclaimed for all the wrong reasons, because it has remained for so long—since 1986!—the hearing world's inevitable standard against which portrayals of major Deaf characters are measured. It appears that Siân Heder's *CODA* has become the new gold standard, but even that is most unfortunate. Yes, there's more Deaf input, but it has become acclaimed for all the wrong reasons. The film has again made it painfully clear how badly we need more Deaf people not only in front of the camera but also *behind* the camera, which is where the true power of accurate representation lies.

HOW I BECAME A BUDDING TV STAR

When a friend emailed me to suggest that I audition for the part of an angry Deaf playwright on *Law & Order: Criminal Intent*, I was bemused. I had done some acting in a film some years before, but I still felt awkward. I never thought of myself as a professional actor. Nevertheless, by that point, I had seen thirteen of my stage plays performed in America and England. I didn't think that gave me enough qualification for the role, however. I happened to be visiting New York City with my then-boyfriend for his mother's seventieth birthday celebration, so it was really a fluke that I *happened* to be in town.

That Saturday, I emailed the casting director with a black-and-white photograph and summarized my background as a playwright. An hour later, she said I was to show up at noon on Monday, and with her email was a PDF of my dialogue. The excerpts gave a bit of background on my character Larry Formosa, along with a scene that I would have to perform.

When my boyfriend and I met with an actress friend of mine, I asked her for advice. She said that there was usually no clear reason why one actor was chosen over another. I realized that whatever I did, I shouldn't take it personally. This was simply a job interview. With that in mind, I studied my lines and thought about my character Larry. In my scene, I was to be rather belligerent toward Goren, Vincent D'Onofrio's character. I had admired Mr. D'Onofrio's previous work in films, so this felt surreal. Me—opposite him? No way.

That Monday I showed up fifteen minutes early. The waiting room was a bleak affair with chairs and some backpacks next to them. A few Deaf actors were also waiting and studying their sides. I thought about why I'd liked certain actors who had auditioned for me, and their self-confidence usually sold me. I decided that I would project self-confidence. Five minutes before noon, an interpreter hired to help with the auditioning process beckoned me. The office was crammed with five people: the director, the producer, the casting director, the interpreter, and a camerawoman. I smiled and I sat down on the couch. The director said, "Why don't you start?"

I went through my lines. He said, "Why don't you make your signs smaller?" I smiled. He had clearly worked with Deaf actors before, because when I worked with them on my DVD projects, they often had to scale down their signs for the camera.

I went through my sides again, thanked them, and left.

I left for Washington, DC the next day. That Thursday, while in DC, I got a barrage of emails from the casting director, the wardrobe supervisor, and friends who had tried to get a hold of me all day. I had won a small part, not as Larry (that part went to Darren Frazier), but as the dean's colleague. (The actress Deanne Bray played the dean.) I returned to New York and showed up early on Monday morning for a ride up north to the Bronx. I was to talk with Deanne on the videophone, but I didn't see any lines in my sides.

The director informed us that we would not be voiced or subtitled. Whatever we said would be accessible only to those who knew ASL. Deanne and I brainstormed about our dialogue, but we were stumped until she brought up a friend's struggles with a hearing ASL beginner student who had almost no facial expressions. It turned out that she had facial Botox injections.

We decided to focus on linguistics and Botox. We did our lines again and again after each camera setup was changed. All of this took about three and half hours. On the night of April 3rd, I showed up on Deanne's videophone: B-O-T-O-X INJECT-FACE FACIAL-EXPRESSION STIFF. It was so trippy to see myself on national television. I was now a budding TV star!

Would I audition for another television program again? Probably not, even though my *Law & Order* experience was great. There are many Deaf actors much more talented than I am, so I was grateful for the experience.

NO MORE SAVAGERY, PLEASE:
ON *THE TRIBE*

Here in America, I've seen firsthand the ways Deaf people are expected to achieve a great many things with their lives, such as becoming business leaders and attorneys. This is par for the course for many of us, which is why we Deaf people often roll our eyes whenever hearing reporters make a point of shoehorning our successes into clichéd "inspiring" stories of a person with a disability "conquering" "against all odds." We all know that the only way anyone wants to succeed, regardless of circumstances, is to stop believing that they are less than the status quo, that they are indeed *already* equal, no matter what anyone says. I'm with the poet Gwendolyn Brooks when she said, "When you use the term 'minority' or 'minorities' in reference to people, you're telling them that they're less than somebody else." This explains why I avoid using the word *minority* when referring to the Deaf community.

Those in hearing society, unfamiliar with what it means to be Deaf, have often proved to be the most significant barrier. I once met a Deaf woman with a PhD who was frustrated in her attempts to find a job in her native Philippines because most people there expected Deaf people—even those with a PhD!—to be good enough only for factory work. And I know of a Deaf man in Brazil whose most pressing goal was to become the manager of a McDonald's because that was the height of the glass ceiling for Deaf people in that country.

So when I first learned about Myroslav Slaboshpytskiy's 2014 Ukrainian film *The Tribe* through the buzz it created at the Cannes Film Festival, I had a number of expectations when it came to seeing Deaf characters in movies. Of course, I'm fully aware that when a Deaf character appears on screen, they are not *me*, but in the eyes of hearing viewers unfamiliar with Deaf culture or the sign language used in the story, they do reflect me in some ways. This is no different from the way gay people felt about seeing themselves portrayed so negatively in movies, usually committing suicide by the film's end, until LGBTQ+ people began to speak up and demand more positive representations in the movies. (Vito Russo's classic *The Celluloid Closet* is uniquely insightful on this topic, and so is the documentary it inspired, directed by Rob Epstein and Jeffrey Friedman.)

What happens in *The Tribe*? In a nutshell, Sergey (Hryhoriy Fesenko), a young Deaf man seemingly of high school age, arrives at a Deaf boarding school. He tries to fit into a group of renegade young Deaf men led by Gera (Alexander Dsiadevich) by engaging in robberies and pimping. When he falls for Anya (Yana Novikova), one of Gera's two concubines, Sergey breaks the rules of "the tribe" with devastating consequences.

The assumptions that a hearing person, uninformed about Deaf people, would be encouraged to make on the basis of this film would naturally be very different from the assumptions that a Deaf viewer would make. This is why, whenever hearing people make films about us, we Deaf people are naturally concerned about whether something on the screen will reflect badly on us. The Deaf community in the United States has been fighting against the closure of Deaf residential schools, which is an important battleground for several reasons. In spite of hearing educators trying to impose the speech-only method of learning on Deaf people, Deaf Americans historically attended state residential schools where they lived together 24/7 (with vacation breaks spent with their families), and in doing so, they bonded together fervently through the commonality of ASL. I remember observing non-signing, hearing parents standing awkwardly next to their Deaf children who had just graduated from Gallaudet, and realizing the degree to which they had only themselves to blame for not learning how to sign. For a Deaf person, a language that's fully accessible is generally more

powerful than ties to a biological family that doesn't make enough
of an effort to include them in the family conversations around
the table. It is through language, not blood, that we feel whole and
connected. In this context, Sergey's desire to be part of a group who
fully understands his language is entirely understandable.

Yet I suspect that for many Deaf Americans still hurting over
the closure of certain Deaf residential schools, it would indeed
prove troubling to watch a group of Deaf teenagers behave so badly
toward each other in this film. In fact, in the dormitory hall in *The
Tribe*, we do not ever see any adult supervision. This is certainly
not how state residential schools for the Deaf are run in America,
which is why I hesitate to make a judgment call on the way the Deaf
school in the film is run. Isn't the presence of a houseparent the
norm for Deaf students after school hours? Or has Slaboshpytskiy
decided to omit their presence for a more dramatic effect? Either
way, the absence of adult supervisors adds to the overall vibe of their
so-called "savagery." This certainly evokes the unsettling ethos that
reigns in Peter Brook's film *Lord of the Flies*, which incidentally does
a better job of exploring the ways in which children who had been
raised to be respectful and considerate can devolve into near-savages
when adults have disappeared from their lives. Because we see how
these schoolboys have tried to behave, we do not initially see them
as savages; certainly not in the same way we might view the primary
Deaf characters in *The Tribe*. Again, this is where subtitles would
have been most helpful.

Anya and Svetka, the two Deaf women in the group (Yana
Novikova and Rosa Babiy), are prostitutes on the side. Gera shows
Sergey how pimping is done in a parking lot amidst large, parked
shipping trucks: knock on the glass of the driver's door and see if
anyone wakes up or comes to the window; if a truck driver shows
interest in having sex, he pays Gera. Then one of the Deaf women
would enter his truck for sex. I find it odd that these two women
seem eager to do this kind of work. This enthusiasm appears to be
more of a wishful stereotype from a (presumably heterosexual) man's
perspective than one grounded in reality; it's my understanding
that prostitution is emotionally exhausting work, especially when
the sex worker must perform for an unattractive client and must
detach themselves emotionally from the sex act in order to function.

I'd like to have learned how these women were initiated into this line of work. Did they not want to participate at first, or had they felt compelled to turn tricks in order to gain acceptance into the "tribe"—the same acceptance that Sergey craved? This is an important question, because so much screen time is given to the women prostituting themselves, compared to attention paid to the male members of "the tribe" engaging in criminal behavior. How were all these members initiated into "the tribe" in the first place?

In this film, almost everyone is exploited, but make no mistake: This is, above all, an exploitation film made by hearing filmmakers. It is useful to ponder what the term truly means, and I quote Wikipedia here:

> Exploitation film is an informal label which may be applied to any film which is generally considered to be low budget, and therefore apparently attempting to gain financial success by "exploiting" a current trend or a niche genre or a base desire for lurid subject matter. The term "exploitation" is common in film marketing for promotion or advertising in any type of film. These films then need something to exploit, such as sex, violence, or romance. An "exploitation film," however, due to its low budget, relies more heavily than usual on "exploitation."[1]

However it may be shot at a cool distance, *The Tribe* has luridness in spades. It would be most interesting to learn what the Ukrainian Deaf community thinks of the film itself, beyond the thrill of seeing their friends up there on the screen.

On a friend's Facebook page, there was a thoughtful discussion of the film, particularly focusing on the absence of adult supervisors in the dormitory. Cynthia Weitzel speculated whether "the absence of supervision possibly represented the absence of human rights in the region, and how it sets the stage for everything that followed." In the discussion, Alicia Lane-Outlaw pointed out that "if this film is indeed an allegory for exploitation of a vulnerable population, the irony is that the film itself exploits a vulnerable population and leaves [the Deaf community] to pick up the pieces."

---

1. https://en.wikipedia.org/wiki/Exploitation_film

——

For hearing people, the notion of silence is powerful. They cannot imagine a world in which they couldn't hear, and if they could imagine such a reality, it's always a world with complete silence. The reality for many Deaf people is quite different; just as deafness can occur across a broad spectrum, so does the perception of silence. Most deaf people have residual hearing to some degree; they can hear some things—just not very well. Silence, at least for me, is not the complete absence of sound that I experience when I turn off my hearing aids (and leave them in my ears), but in the lack of motion around me. Seeing a flicker of light in my peripheral vision, even in a quiet room, does not represent silence for me; in fact, it's quite annoying. It's just as bad as hearing a jackhammer pounding from across the street.

At one point in *The Tribe*, a huge truck runs over a Deaf character, who is standing with his back to the truck. The incident is totally unbelievable because the scene is predicated on a *hearing* person's concept of silence in the framework of deafness. In the few minutes before the incident happens, we see the truck's front lights hitting the pavement in front of the Deaf character's feet. He would have turned around a lot more quickly at that moment, but he didn't. (Many Deaf people, after having seen the film, told me that they couldn't believe the character did not feel the weight and vibration on the pavement from such a heavy truck. Incidentally, the character's death did not seem to have any emotional consequences for Sergey, let alone "the tribe." Exploitation, anyone?) The takeaway from this particular scene can only be that it is truly dangerous to be Deaf.

Furthermore, at one point, Sergey enters two rooms. In the first room, he commits a truly shocking act; in the second room, he does it again. I find it totally unbelievable that none of the Deaf people sleeping in these rooms responded to the vibrations created by Sergey's actions. Moreover, some Deaf people awaken without quite knowing why when someone enters their room; the person can exude a very subtle odor that a sleeping person can detect immediately even if they don't hear a thing. (It's not clear whether a Deaf consultant was involved with the making of this film, but this is a perfect example of why having a Deaf consultant on location would have been incredibly useful to increase plausibility in such scenes.)

In *The Guardian*, Peter Bradshaw raises an interesting question about silence as a motif in this film:

> The main question is: signing is a language like any other, so why not have subtitles? How is our experience of this different from any foreign-language movie without subtitles? The point, I think, is that their silence underscores their alienation from us. They are a different tribe: outside the law, below the salt. And their silence has something to do with the criminal code of omertà: you don't talk.[2]

In spite of my objections to the way Deaf characters are portrayed in the film, I will give Slaboshpytskiy credit for not showing Deaf characters in social isolation. (There is an unsettling exception in which a student with Down syndrome is rejected by everyone; even more surprising is that Sergey is upset at being thrown into the Down syndrome student's room. Sergey, who himself was rejected, reveals his ableist bent here.) Nevertheless, Deaf people are certainly capable of having many friends. I don't know about you, but if you've ever paid close attention to groups of Deaf people signing, you've noticed how much they *love* to talk. It's as if their hands can't shut up, and it's absolutely wonderful! And seeing them sign away without encumbrance to anyone is pure bliss for my eyes. It isn't just because I am fluent in ASL, but because I personally know how much of an emotional price each of us Deaf people has had to pay in order to find a home in each other's hands, especially those of us with hearing parents who do not bother to sign. Deaf viewers watching *The Tribe* will appreciate, on a basic level, why the main character Sergey would seek acceptance by the group. Yet the film fails to address its story's weakest aspect: If these people had behaved so atrociously toward Sergey mainly because he had fallen in love with Anya, then why doesn't he instead attempt to connect with other Deaf people outside the "tribe"? We catch brief glimpses of other Deaf people of all ages on the periphery of the story, especially in the scene where many Deaf people around their age witness a fight

---

2. Peter Bradshaw, "Review of The Tribe, by Miroslav Slaboshpitsky," *Guardian*, May 14, 2015, https://www.theguardian.com/film/2015/may/14/the-tribe-review

between Sergey and another character, so he'd surely have known that there are many kinds of Deaf people in the community. Why couldn't he go to them for help? If he is seeking a familial connection, a familial acceptance, which I suspect he is, why doesn't he go back to the principal, or other Deaf people in the film? That his hopes to be accepted by the rejecting "tribe" seem incredibly myopic makes him less of a hero. Subtitles would've helped clarify such nuances and motives in the storyline and would have made the characters seem more like the human beings that they surely are.

Sergey rarely gets what he wants in this film; there is no room for him to maneuver. In fact, he's quite passive in accepting the demands made of him, even when it becomes degrading, as when he catches Anya and a customer in the act. To make a story compelling, its main character must win some, lose some, capped by an ending somehow making a point that the film has been building toward all along. To give you an idea of how relentless its grimness is, I clocked the first time I caught sight of a genuine smile—about sixty-two minutes into the film! I find *The Tribe* to be the most depressing piece of filmmaking I've seen in decades. (I used to think of Sydney Pollack's film *They Shoot Horses, Don't They?* as the most depressing film of all time. Not anymore.)

We have the civil rights movement to thank, in part, for creating the national awareness of how Black people are portrayed in film, so we are certainly more sensitive to racism in the cultural arena today compared to days gone by. (For instance, today no one could get away with the blatant racism and glorification of the Ku Klux Klan that D. W. Griffith depicted in his 1915 silent film *Birth of a Nation*, a huge moneymaker. Unfortunately, racism still exists, so we have a long way to go.)

Yet hearing reviewers, almost without exception, do not realize how audist *The Tribe* is.

What is *audism*? The word was coined by Tom Humphries in 1975, and Wikipedia defines it best:

> Audism is the notion that one is superior based on one's ability to hear or to behave in the manner of one who hears, or **that**

life without hearing is futile and miserable, or an attitude based on pathological thinking which results in a negative stigma toward anyone who does not hear. (emphasis mine)[3]

Before I delve further into *The Tribe*, I want to point out a major factor that has often, unfortunately, motivated many hearing filmmakers to create stories about us Deaf people: novelty. Examples abound everywhere, but I'll stick to only one: Hearing nonsigners focus on learning dirty signs in ASL online, and in one notorious case, a hearing signer has tried to profit from teaching just those signs even though many of her renditions aren't linguistically correct. Because hearing nonsigners think it's absolutely hilarious that certain signs show this or that aspect considered "dirty," the result is that they are encouraged to think of ASL as a punch line and nothing more. It doesn't matter if they sign a dirty word in an incorrect way, in much the same way that some people might mispronounce certain words; so can nonsigners misform their signs. In fact, they usually do, and they have no idea of the degree to which they are embarrassing themselves. They are not taught to respect the language, nor do they know that in America, the Deaf community nearly lost ASL due to the concerted efforts by hearing educators and the medical establishment to oppress our language in favor of speech, and that countless Deaf people have paid an enormous price for the right to use their mother tongue. This fact is very important to acknowledge when learning ASL. With this in mind, it will be most instructive to see what Myroslav Slaboshpytskiy had to say about why he made this film. The following quote comes directly from the film's press release materials:

I was thinking about making such a movie 20 years ago. By all means, this is an homage to silent film, where actors were communicating through pantomime. I know, such movies are produced almost every year, successfully or not. However all works I've seen are following the silent movie stylization. For me, the main goal was to make a more realistic, natural silent film, which would be **easily understood without words**. The

---

3. Wikipedia no longer uses this longer definition; it is defined as "discrimination against Deaf/deaf people." https://en.wikipedia.org/wiki/Audism

thing is, nowadays there are lots of films, especially TV ones, which you can just listen. An audience is used to that. On the other hand there are films, where all actors stay silent all the time. I've made a silent short film myself. But now, with *The Tribe*, I've found another path, unique and suitable for my film. Sign language is like **a dance, ballet, pantomime, kabuki theater, etc.** At the same time, there's no grotesque in it—people are communicating that way for real. Besides, according to recent developments in medicine, sign language will be a dead language in perspective. In some time it will cease to exist at all. But I find sign language **fascinating**, and I really wanted to **share this feeling with the audience.**" (emphases mine)

Silent films have always fascinated me. One might think that because sound is not required to enjoy these films, it's ideal for Deaf people. There is that, yes, but I enjoy silent films for a very different reason. As a Deaf writer who straddles both worlds of English and hearing culture on one hand, and ASL and Deaf culture on the other, I am naturally obsessed with language and its power to transform. Therefore, the language of cinema in all its infancy is right there before us, and yet it's exciting to catch the subtle shifts in syntax. Filmmakers are learning how to write the language of light fluently with each shot, each cut, each scene. They are so captivated by this process that they do not always check their racism, sexism, and xenophobia that can be at work when they frame their stories and particularly when they tell actors to perform in a certain way; those in power are accustomed to never having their "-isms" questioned.

I'd like to quote Slaboshpytskiy again (please note the phrase "deaf and dumb"—like "deaf mute"—is an unacceptable term in America):

It's been my old dream to do homage to the silent movie. To make a film that can be understood without a single voiced word. It's not that I was thinking about some kind of a European "existential" movie in which the heroes would keep silence throughout half the film. And besides, actors were not silent in the silent movie. They communicated very actively through a wealth of byplay and body language. They could communicate emotions and feelings without a line to say. And it is not by incident that most of silent movie stars had come from the pantomime. This is exactly why I've always wanted to shoot a film about the life of deaf-and-dumb people. With no speech and with no subtitles. And with the participation of real deaf-and-dumb people.

It's clear that he seems to have confused sign language with pantomime. Almost any sign language may appear to be pantomime to the uninformed eye, but it is indeed not; it is a foreign language in its own right, complete with vocabulary, syntax, and idioms. Pantomime does not require the knowledge of signs to be understood. If sign language were truly pantomime, as Slaboshpytskiy seems to have implied here, then why was I unable to follow the "pantomimes" in his film? Incidentally, the only time that I felt I understood what was being said in Ukrainian Sign Language was when the woodwork teacher (Alexander Panivan) instructed his students about safety measures in his classroom prior to the camera pulling back to reveal the students sanding down their own wooden hammers. The light was clear, and the context was clear.

There is also another story that's readily apparent but not always articulated when talking about silent films, and that is how the vaudevillian style of acting began to transform itself into a more naturalistic style. When the nickelodeons began to catch on, vaudeville performers onstage had been accustomed to projecting their voices and gestures without the aid of microphones to the farthest reaches of a theater, so when they began to perform before the loud cameras, they, too, assumed that they had to act the same way with their bodies. Then filmmakers, having tired of shooting scenes as if capturing the action all at once, as if onstage, began to experiment with the notion of cutting together two different shots to say something different. Context became even more crucial. Suddenly, close-ups of actors performing in the vaudevillian style of acting began to look ridiculous. Such unnatural performing became even more distracting with technological advancements in both cameras and lights, combined with a stronger appreciation of lighting techniques, and actors began to tone down their oversized expressions. They began to look less like two-dimensional characters and to behave more like real people.

All this brings me to another major issue I have with *The Tribe*: With very few exceptions, nearly all the scenes are shot from a certain distance, as if this were intended to be an homage to the early days of cinema. Many scenes aren't lit very well, and in fact, some scenes show Deaf characters signing from behind. Regardless of whether we know their language, we cannot see *what* they are signing. This is comparable to listening to a voice-over track with phrases and sentences fuzzed over here and there; you cannot quite follow what is being said. That nothing is voiced or subtitled in the film at all is an admirable concept that the Deaf community would love to see more of, if only to redress the fact that so many hearing films are inaccessible to us, but in this case, it doesn't work. The "fascinating" aspect of seeing a sign language we don't know, on top of having been shot in such a way that often prevents seeing the hands of the person signing, only contributes to the film's novelty factor; nay, it becomes part of that long tradition of hearing filmmakers always in search of the exotic, the freaky: "Look at these people signing! We don't know what the hell they are saying, but it looks so *fascinating* [a word Slaboshpytskiy used himself]. Let's watch and try to figure out what they are saying." As a result, those of us who don't know Ukrainian Sign Language are forced to make a lot of assumptions while watching the story. (No, sign language is most assuredly not universal; in fact, many countries have their own sign languages.) If Slaboshpytskiy wanted to make a film that "would be easily understood without words"—his words again—he has failed miserably in this attempt.

I have been using ASL for over thirty years, long enough to have been exposed to a wide variety of comments and attitudes about sign language, and one of them—"a dance, ballet, pantomime, kabuki theater," quoting Slaboshpytskiy here—is a common remark made by hearing people. For us signers, a sign language is not so much a ballet or pantomime; it is a bona fide *language*, just like any other. I once met a hearing stage director who had the mistaken concept of having Deaf characters talk onstage and move fluidly, rather like ballet dancers, at the same time. I asked her if she wanted Deaf audience members to be able to comprehend these performers onstage. "Yes, of course," she said. "Then they need to stand or walk slowly," I said, "because we need to *see* what they are saying. No shoulders blocking the signs." She still didn't quite understand my objection. I responded by stretching the syllables with my voice: "*Ooooh, this is soooo great that weeee arrrrre talkinggggg soooo beeeeeooootifullyyyy*. The English sounds atrocious, right? But you seem to want to do the same thing to ASL." My explanation upset her, partly because I was ruining her director's "vision" (and dismantling one of her misconceptions about sign language), but I had to remind her that as long as she didn't know ASL herself, it would be incredibly presumptuous of her to have any authority over the "elocution" of ASL if she expected full accessibility for the entire audience.

I was reminded of her when I watched how the signers were staged in *The Tribe*. I don't get the sense that Slaboshpytskiy truly cared about full information accessibility here; most, if not all, Deaf filmmakers would have framed this film very differently. One of the things I love most about the Deaf community is how important it is to have everything clear and accessible no matter the form. Sometimes, it's a matter of better lighting, a quieter corner, or writing back and forth on a notepad (some people text instead for conversations). It's the same with films, which is why foreign films with subtitles are such a godsend; in a way, these subtitles bring d/ Deaf audience members to the same level as hearing people who don't know the language being spoken in the film.

I'd like to make one other remark about the distance between the performers and the camera. In the early days of silent cinema, the static wide shots were a necessity for two reasons: The cameras back then were huge and heavy, and they required a lot of light. That is no longer true, and I recall a few scenes in *The Tribe* where the camera was handheld. But that's not my focus here. Part of my problem with the film stems not only from the fact that its characters are two-dimensional, as in either good or bad, with no in-between or emotional complexity, but also that we, as audience members, are rarely permitted to come closer and absorb their faces, the inner essence of their being, long enough to feel a kinship, a deeper empathy. I'm aware that my expectations as a filmgoer have been shaped by American and Western European films, which are shot and edited differently, and that this technique of keeping a certain distance between camera and character is considered a hallmark of Eastern

European cinema, but there's something else to consider: Distance is a very powerful tool in the language of film—and in society itself. I'm much more interested in the latter for a simple reason. In the 1970s, when gay people in America were being ostracized for demanding equality on the legal front, Harvey Milk shared a very simple idea that was pure genius: "Come out to everyone you know." Why is that idea so powerful? Because it forced family, friends, and coworkers to stop seeing gay people as evil, easily portrayed from a distance in the media by homophobic conservatives, and begin seeing them as *people* just like other friends, neighbors, coworkers, and family members. Once that started happening, heterosexuals began to examine their own homophobia and created a ripple effect that hasn't stopped spreading outward ever since. I thought about this a great deal while watching *The Tribe*. Because we are not allowed to come closer and know these characters as people, the impression of these Deaf characters as "savages" remains far too pungent. (In some underlit scenes, I couldn't figure out which character was which because they were all wearing black! Thus, the raves over Valentyn Vasyanovych's cinematography puzzled me.) As long as a great deal of misinformation about Deaf people continues to exist out there, the Deaf community has every right to be concerned about how they are portrayed. Once committed to film, a misinformed portrayal is there forever to be seen and replicated (consciously or not), which explains why so many hearing screenwriters have perpetuated stereotypes about Deaf (and disabled) characters in their own work. Most hearing writers these days have thankfully become sensitive about the need to strive for accuracy in cultural representations of communities not their own, which is why they often do their homework when crafting their stories. As much as I applaud Slaboshpytskiy for "listening" to the Ukrainian Deaf community and incorporating some of their stories into his script, it is indeed unfortunate that his audist bias comes through loud and clear: Deaf people are best appreciated from a distance. They are not truly people; just savages reduced to their basic survival needs. This impression is deepened by the fact that the film is not subtitled. Having members of any community reduced to two-dimensional characters is never a good excuse to call a film "powerful," especially when it reinforces the concept that "life without hearing is futile and miserable," as Wikipedia has so defined audism.

In order to combat audism in their work, hearing filmmakers and producers must be willing to seek far more input from Deaf consultants, especially where signers are framed for maximum legibility. Having the bottom space of their signing cut off is akin to hearing a person speak and having her voice suddenly cut off in mid-sentence for no reason whatsoever. An editor truly familiar with the sign language used in a film would know where to make the cuts, as opposed to cutting because it looks "better." Such botched cuts and badly framed shots of signers are among the hallmarks of hearing filmmakers solely interested in the novelty of using Deaf characters in their work and nothing more. They may claim to be genuinely interested in working with Deaf people in their projects, but as long as Deaf people and consultants are not given equal voice in the process, these hearing filmmakers would be rightly accused of inflicting their audist and ableist bias. The bottom line with *The Tribe*: A hearing person wrote and directed a film about Deaf people much in the same way that a White person might have made a film about Black people a century ago. I wonder how the African-American community would feel if the Deaf characters in *The Tribe* were replaced with hearing Black characters whose speech wasn't clear at all without any other change in the script. The story would be considered racist because they have been reduced to savages who don't know any better. So why is it more acceptable to portray Deaf characters in this light?

Thus it has been incredibly puzzling that this film won film festival awards. Obviously, the voters were most likely hearing, but three reasons do come to mind.

The first reason: novelty. Look, Ma—no subtitles, no voiceovers, no music! It may prove enlightening to look at what some hearing reviewers have said about the film. Peter Bradshaw, writing about the film for *The Guardian*, said:

> . . . all the rows and confrontations are conducted in sign language, and this is what accompanies the fistfights—there are no subtitles, no intertitles, no explanations. And there is no orchestral soundtrack or incidental music. The whole thing

happens in eerie quiet, **as if on another planet**: it is like a nature documentary with the sound turned down. The film unfolds to the continuous accompaniment of shoes squeaking and shuffling on lino floors, in squalid institutional dorm corridors where the doors open outward, like animal cages. **There are inchoate non-verbal whispers, or grunts and gasps of anger and pain.** I couldn't help remembering the quotation attributed to Nietzsche about dancers being thought insane by those who can't hear the music. (Emphases mine)[4]

Justin Chang of *Variety* remarked that "we could be watching a bizarre dance performance as enacted by a silent flash mob." But Tomas Hachard of *Slant Magazine* makes an interesting point:

That Slaboshpytskiy ultimately succeeds at keeping us engaged doesn't, however, do away with the problems of making the audience approach these characters through such a layer of incomprehension. . . . **The film never entirely justifies why those who can't read sign language must experience the story so differently from how the characters live it.** It never quite brushes off the obvious question of why, in the effort of putting a marginalized set of characters on screen, we should limit our understanding of them. (Emphasis mine)[5]

Jordan Hoffman wrote in *BadAss Digest*:

The gals don't *seem* to be upset about their exploitation. They get gifts, like cheap, tacky souvenir T-shirts when another older guy comes back from a trip to Rome. We're conditioned to think of these women as victims, but since we only *somewhat* understand what they're saying, it's harder to know how they feel—**harder to know what's a face for others, since we rarely see anyone by themselves** . . . Slaboshpytskiy's decision to keep everything at a remove may be seen as overkill for a movie that

---

4. Bradshaw, "Review of The Tribe."
5. Tomas Hachard, "Toronto International Film Festival: Myroslav Slaboshpytskiy's The Tribe," *Slant*, September 10, 2014. https://www.slantmagazine.com/film/toronto-film-review-the-tribe/

is already intentionally distancing, but it enhances the notion that everything you are seeing is in some weird, far away universe. . . . One lengthy scene—something of a *Fight Club* moment—has a scuffle in the foreground and a gaggle of kids watching on the side of some industrial hill. The assembled crowd is all furiously communicating with one another, and the sequence goes on for so long that it extends beyond being an ethnographic film. **It becomes a peek at something unusual in nature.** I don't want to sound flippant, but the image is so unpredictable that **to my untrained eye it felt like watching a cordoned-off area in a zoo.** I know this may read as cruel, but that isn't my intention. From a purely visual point of view, it is **a stretched-out glimpse at humans behaving in a way I've never really seen before.** (Emphases mine)[6]

For *Indiewire*, Eric Kohn said:

By avoiding closeups, **the filmmaker makes it clear that their entire bodies define their identities.** . . . Since Sergey can't speak for himself, many scenes are dominated by precise details, particularly those including explicit sex. These aren't the only blatant instances of shock value as the plot grows steadily darker, sometimes to the detriment of material that already holds enough appeal without the added subversive edge. However, **the use of sexuality as a storytelling device has a certain underlying narrative power, rendering these seemingly foreign characters—at least for anyone unable to comprehend their works—in intimate details. Already using their bodies to communicate, their only mode of communication takes on its rawest manifestation when they're frolicking in the nude.** (Emphases mine)[7]

In *Film Comment*, Jonathan Romney concludes his review with this statement: "Silence never felt so savage."

6. Jordan Hoffman, "Cannes Review: The Tribe Is Unlike Anything Else," *BadAss Digest*, May 22, 2014. https://birthmoviesdeath.com/2014/05/22/cannes-review-the-tribe-is-unlike-anything-else
7. Eric Kohn, "Review: Sign Language Drama 'The Tribe' Is an Unprecedented Cinematic Accomplishment," IndieWire, May 22, 2014. https://www.indiewire.com/2014/05/review-sign-language-drama-the-tribe-is-an-unprecedented-cinematic-accomplishment-26188/

The second reason for the praise the film has received is the unchallenged concept of "normal." Most hearing people have always seen people with disabilities as somehow less than them; therefore, any film that reinforces this ableist view, however subtly or unintentionally, is always a good thing, especially when a disabled character "conquers" her own disability; and it is all the more inspiring when the action is portrayed by an able-bodied performer. How many Academy Awards have been bestowed on such performances? In this case, however, the Deaf characters in *The Tribe* are played by Deaf actors performing for the first time. As long as hearing (and able-bodied) filmmakers continue to believe that their way of thinking is considered "normal," that their own existence trumps anyone else's way of living, they will continue to consider it their birthright to make films about Deaf (and disabled) people even if it perpetuates their audist (and ableist) bias, which in turn hurts the Deaf (and disability) community in the long run.

The concept of "normal" is dangerous because it's the root of audism, homophobia, racism, and so on. The Greek philosopher Aristotle believed that if a deaf person couldn't speak, it was because they had substandard intelligence. That misconception alone had set deaf people back for centuries, and it wasn't until Charles-Michel de l'Épée had the seemingly radical idea of educating deaf people not through speech, but through their native sign language in Paris, France, that such prejudices subsided at all. Deaf people were suddenly proven to be educable and far more intelligent than anyone had imagined.

And the third reason for the film's critical success is that it contains a few scenes that are truly gut-wrenching to watch. There is a scene involving an abortion in a woman's kitchen. The abortionist, who knows signs, takes a gnarly rope hanging from outside the kitchen window and fashions it in such a way that both ends have a loop. The pregnant Deaf woman sits on the counter and lifts one foot through the loop, slides the rope behind her neck, and slips her foot through the other loop. There she is, curled up like an animal yet with her knees up in the air, awaiting the abortionist to do her work, which she does. (This is one of the few times when I was grateful for the distance between camera and action.) The entire scene, from arrival to the apartment to the kitchen and the abortion

NO MORE SAVAGERY, PLEASE | 141

itself, was shot impressively in a single take. When the deed is done, the abortionist leaves the kitchen without asking if she is all right, and the Deaf woman breaks down in sobs. To my recollection, it's the only time we hear a Deaf person use her voice in the film. A Deaf filmmaker once shared her belief with me that if Marlee Matlin hadn't suddenly used her voice when she argued with William Hurt for the last time in the Randa Haines film *Children of a Lesser God*, she wouldn't have won her Oscar. She could've signed gibberish even if her lines were voiced by Mr. Hurt. I imagine that Ms. Matlin's speech in real life wouldn't be perfect, therefore seeing a beautiful woman unleashing her angry, animal-sounding voice for the first time—and in the film's final confrontation at that!—must've been quite a considerable jolt for the voting members of the Academy.

Perhaps it's no surprise that *The Tribe* is getting attention because savagery, especially when reduced to silence and mystery, seems powerful, almost noble.

ON STEVE JOBS

Without Steve Jobs, who had just passed away while I was writing this book, I wouldn't be where I am today.

I've never met the man. The avalanche of tributes pouring down since he passed away underlines his most singular achievement: He made the concept that computers *had* to be easy to use by the non-techies—otherwise known as "the rest of us"—a viable reality, and in doing so, changed the course of human history. Given how paramount computers—whether they be sitting on our desks or resting in our hands—have become in our daily lives, this feat alone has made him the most important person from the last quarter-century. Hyperbole? I don't think so. His insistence on a better user experience on the Macintosh spread not only throughout Apple, the company he co-founded, but throughout the streets of Silicon Valley, Redmond, and beyond.

I used to be a hardcore Microsoftie. In fact, I used to mock the Macheads throughout the 1990s. I couldn't understand their passion for a computer that was outrageously overpriced. What was wrong with them? Then, along came the advent of an affordable video format: the mini-DV tape. Such video cameras were steadily dropping in price, but what blew me away was the *quality* of work possible with a prosumer (pro[fessional] + [con]sumer = prosumer) camera. When I first saw the quality of mini-DV footage, a light bulb went on in my head. Finally, I thought, independent Deaf filmmakers could make movies for a minimum amount of money. The costs of developing a lab print of footage shot on film were so prohibitive that the reality of the mini-DV format seemed like an impossible miracle.

Then came my next question. Could it be edited cheaply? At the time, no. I'd read of indie filmmakers shoring their savings just to buy a single Avid workstation for $30,000 and scheduling their editing times so they couldn't overlap each other with their projects. I was crestfallen. It didn't make sense to have an expensive nonlinear editing solution for a fairly cheap video format. Nevertheless, I realized that if I wanted to make movies, I needed to learn how to use the Mac. Everyone had said so. I decided to begin with my first iMac in the spring of 1999. Initially, it was a struggle to understand an entirely different operating system, but after a few months, I "got it." I bought my first mini-DV camera (Sony VX-2000) and began shooting. I learned how to edit using iMovie, and then when Steve Jobs announced Final Cut Pro (FCP) for $1K, I was astounded. Apple was clearly taking on Avid. In a matter of a few years, the number of Avid editing houses dropped dramatically in half.

Learning how to edit video changed me. I felt suddenly empowered in ways I didn't expect. I didn't have to wait for a professional to put together a video for me. I could just jump right in and teach myself how to edit on FCP, thank you very much. I ended up shooting, directing, and editing two DVDs for the Tactile Mind Press. It wasn't long before I felt confident enough to design and set up websites for clients, as well as do freelance graphic design. In short, I wasn't just a writer anymore. Everything about the image entranced me. Decades of absorbing all kinds of art in galleries and museums had paid off for the inner artist in me. I could articulate myself far more visually than I'd thought possible.

Would I have accomplished as much had I stayed with using a Windows machine? Highly unlikely. The ease of the Mac had enabled me to feel empowered to take on a lot of creative risks without feeling the fear of having the computer crap out on me like my Windows machines always had. For that, I have to thank Steve Jobs. Granted, he wasn't the first to do so, but he and his team at Apple did make it a lot easier for us to explore the idea of making music and recording podcasts on our own, burning DVDs of our videos, creating glossy books filled with our favorite photographs, and so on. *We* could make ourselves heard in ways that we couldn't on television and radio. Every time Steve Jobs took the stage to announce a much-rumored new product, it was always exciting because he held the promise of our first peek of the future to come. But he's gone. He will soon become a marker of our shared past. We are now the future. We must realize that about ourselves. We must look at ourselves in the mirror. It is up to us to make the future far more exciting and glorious than he'd ever dreamed. His staggering successes—in spite of the unceremonious flops he'd suffered—remind us how important it is to be less afraid of taking risks and trying again even if we do fail. Because when we do finally succeed, we may find ourselves changing the world in the most surprising ways.

IN THE YEAR 2122

In the year 2122, the Deaf person will be virtually unrecognizable. This is not a fantasy of mine, but deducible from a series of facts based on the inevitable progress of technological advances. Due to the relentless government cuts in education budgets, residential schools for the Deaf will have become a footnote in the tumultuous history of education in America and all across the world. What has happened is that, thanks to cheap digital video technology and broadband access, Deaf students all over the world are able to attend classes together online. They can raise their hands to their teacher and be seen by their classmates as raising their hand; maybe they'll sign to each other privately when the teacher looks down to type something on her keyboard to show a new example.

Heck, right now it's possible for students—hearing or Deaf—to learn individually at their own pace and not have to be in the same "room" at the same time. Virtual learning is only starting!

This will also mean that like English, ASL—or actually a polyglot of signs borrowed from other sign languages around the world due to the intense interactions via the internet, accelerated rather than accumulated over centuries as English had been—will become the dominant sign language for the global Deaf community. Many of the colorful stories behind each sign in each country will be retained in a permanent digital medium, thanks to the efforts of concerned linguists, and archived online. Deaf children will be able to access these resources and "read" generations of stories originally captured on nitrate, celluloid, and analog videotape, and then transferred preciously and permanently in a digital form.

Libraries, as we know them, will be very different. Books, with their sweetly faded glory, will still strike a powerful siren of nostalgia in our souls, and they will continue to inspire intense debates about the future of printed books in conferences and in "real" bookstores around the country. But due to the staggering deficit carried over too many generations, the government will be forced to cut down on the cost of maintaining books in their traditional physical form. People will still be able to borrow ebooks—hundreds of pages downloaded in a flash of milliseconds, actually—into paper-thin, breezy, and portable ereaders graced with screens that mimic the appearance of paper and yet are readable in natural sunlight or artificial light. When readers are done, they click on a button or two, and the book has been returned automatically. Because of this, publishers have discovered that the long-held assumptions about demographics and marketability are no longer true; for example, a lot more people than originally thought are truly interested in Greek philosophy and Deaf culture of the late twentieth century. And there will be an International Bestseller List, generated by the number of downloads per new and long-standing title, which will no longer be dictated by the *New York Times*.

Historically, the number of people who want to "cure" deafness and do away with silly notions of Deaf culture have always outnumbered the signing Deaf community and its supporters. This is the main reason why—especially with the amazing and mind-boggling advances made in both medical science and technology—I have said that in the year of 2122, the Deaf person will be virtually unrecognizable.

Even ASL interpreters will be a thing of the past once all the problems involved with sound and phonetic recognition by computers are solved; that is, a portable and light computer described previously could replace the interpreter's function with instant captions. In fact, there will be no need for interpreters of any kind because such transliterations—and translations from one language to another—will be taken completely for granted. This also means that every single movie will be completely accessible, doing away with agencies that specialize in subtitling and closed-captioning. And, of course, all this means that the Deaf person must rely more on English.

I seriously doubt that the Deaf person in the year 2122 will have as much a problem with English—or any other language, for that matter—because of the automatic acceptance of caption computers from day one of detection in the same way that hearing aids are mandated after audiological evaluation. This will remove much of the misunderstanding that occurs in lipreading. Because of the technological advances made in every field, the concept of a eight-hour-a-day workweek will be changed to five hours a day; parents will have fewer excuses to neglect their children, more so when many schools online would require their parents to participate in their children's learning processes. Likewise, it would be very natural for parents of babies who are deaf to want to learn ASL early on because by then, everyone will understand that being d/Deaf is no big deal. Actually, technological ineptness will be much more of a "handicap."

The internet will enable the sheer dissemination of information about deafness and culture so as to be instantly available to anyone who types in the search word "deafness." After all, everyone will think nothing of calling their friends in France or India to ask their advice on their Deaf children in the same way we used to visit our next-door neighbors to borrow a cup of sugar. (Of course, the fact remains that all researchers and corporations founded on cochlear implants have been long bankrupt after a series of staggering lawsuits—all questioning the wrongful assumptions made in the name of language acquisition and medical science. By that time, there will be only three people left in the world who are forced due to medical complications to wear cochlear implants.)

This global thinking alone means that everyone will have to accept the wild divergence of cultural beliefs and "differentness" as a matter of course in the same way that New Yorkers today often accept others not of their own kind as a matter of course. This also means that as we get to know our own neighbors, we realize that they are actually *people*, not some immigrant family with strange clothes and accents. This kind of thinking would also lead to wars between groups rather than entire countries as demonstrated way too often in the course of history.

———

The affordability of video-related technology will mean that Hollywood as we know it will be gone. There will always be stars—it's self-evident in our human nature that we will continue to need such mythic figures to help replace our loss of belief in institutionalized religions—but the digital film industry will no longer be controlled singularly by the media hype of Hollywood.

Marginalized communities will find themselves able to afford low-end computers that are generations better than the most expensive computer available for home use today. Suddenly, the notion of media representation is right in their hands, and with that, the Deaf community will realize that lobbying and being ignored in the media aren't enough, so they will concentrate on making movies about their cultural histories and about the concerns that mark their communities.

Deaf filmmakers will be the norm in the community; in fact, there won't be enough Deaf actors skilled in ASL to go around, and the Deaf film—and theatrical—community will seem more like a huge repertory company. Because there are so few Deaf people skilled in sign language (due to early detection and all of the above), hearing children of Deaf parents will actually be cast in Deaf roles due to the intense popularity of other Deaf actors (currently filming or performing in a stage play being digital filmed for online consumption). Deaf filmmakers will marvel at the very notion that a century before, Deaf performers had to fight for the right to audition for Deaf characters in the film industry; they will wish that every one of them were alive to be in their movies. There will be many Deaf stars, and Marlee Matlin will scarcely be remembered in the minds of Deaf children growing up on a bumper crop of movies made by Deaf filmmakers.

Bypassing the often-questionable artistic tastes of many film distributors, the internet will have become the main medium of advertising and publicity; any movie lover will of course request information about new digital films available for downloading and streaming. It will be possible for Deaf social clubs to gather together in large living rooms around the world to watch the same "internet premiere" of a new Deaf film. Afterwards, Deaf viewers can commingle "in person" and via the internet all around the world, sharing their reactions to the film just shown. The American

Academy Awards will no longer have the same magic; each country will have been savvy enough to capitalize on promoting their own version of the Oscar online. The global rethinking of the movie lover will give birth to a new breed of digital film observer: Once interested in only the Academy Awards and the choices made at the Cannes Film Festival, the movie award fanatic will be able to "attend" all these ceremonies around the world via the Internet and take their virtual friends with them for the ride, sharing their snide remarks and nods of appreciation with each other via tweets and elsewhere on social media. The Academy Awards will actually be degraded as too "elitist."

Does that mean the spell of film would be entirely gone in the year 2122?

I should hope not. We very much need to mythologize, and that's why stars still have such commanding presence, even in an era when everyone keeps saying that overbloated and overbudgeted films will really kill the freestanding studio system. In spite of staggering profits, Hollywood's financial management is anything but sound. The metaphor of the movie studio industry precariously located close to the San Andreas Fault couldn't be more apt.

The digital film will give rise to a very different sort of Deaf literature, long precluded to the debates back in the 1980s; the cost factor of preservation compared to the expense of analog video will be next to zero. In fact, because of the cheapness of technology itself, there will be way *too* much of it as there will be too many—and most likely shoddy—digital films made by people, both Deaf and hearing, who haven't taken the time to study great cinematic classics. The same thing has already happened when computers became affordable for home use and when people thought that because they were able to use it, they could think of themselves as "writers" when they hadn't even really learned how to analyze the work of great writers in order to learn how to improve their own craft. Such a glut will become a serious problem, but on the whole, this will mean a truer democratization of self-expression previously unimaginable.

All this means, I guess, is that the eye will become even more crucial to the literature of the future. Deaf filmmakers will be uniquely qualified not because of their understanding of ASL but because their work will be taken seriously like anyone else's, so much to the point that people—after watching all sorts of foreign films—keep forgetting they are watching a Deaf movie.

The cheapness of digital film means that theater will be staged not just for the audience but also for preservation on digital film. Because of the sheer diffusion of acting opportunities in these non-union films, actors are actually able to make a decent living from performing in all sorts of digital films. Casting directors, producers, and others in the digital film industry will not only have the image of a potential star but also a compact compilation of that performer's work.

All that would mean is that ASL may no longer be considered as *the* crucial barometer for acceptance into the Deaf community. The smallness of the global Deaf community (compared to the numbers today) by the year 2122 will force Deaf people to bond together in greater numbers like a huge family across boundaries designated by mapmakers and wars, to meet potential mates for marriage.

What will still count, though, are the shared experiences of being unable to participate as fully in spite of all the technological advances. People will want to be away from computers just to be with each other in the old-fashioned sense, to see beyond the lifelike 3-D renderings of friends on the monitor for the actual touch, for the irreplaceable sensation of a heart-to-heart hug. Deaf people will still continue to move as adults to cities where they can congregate and spend time with each other in this world—and most likely carry on the same old feuds among themselves as they always have—but they will no longer feel powerless to effect change in their own lives. The only thing stopping them will be themselves alone. (Come to think of it, that's very true *today*.)

The tremendous social changes wrought by the computer in our lives today are only a tiny foreshadowing of what will come. The more I reflect on the future, the more I realize that the internet-based computer—more than anything else—will actually aid in the future of the Deaf community's struggle for understanding and acceptance. The concept of information inaccessibility will be gone, and the Deaf person in the eyes of the global community will be accepted just like anybody else.

By then being Deaf—and whatever ethnic differences we are blessed with—will be no big deal, and that's what I hope will happen in the year 2122.

LEARNING TO BREATHE

Yesterday afternoon, I took the elevator down from my apartment to my trusty bicycle. When I unlocked my bike, I realized that I'd forgotten to take along my helmet and gloves. I debated going back upstairs, but I decided that I would do what I'd always done when I was growing up in Ironwood and biking on my secondhand ten-speed all over town: No helmet or gloves would do. I hadn't done that in years. I had long waited for the weather in Minneapolis to warm up enough for a leisurely bike ride around the Chain of Lakes (Lake of the Isles, Lake Bde Maka Ska, and Lake Harriet are all connected via bike trails), and the sun's warmth seemed fortuitous, precious even.

With Sia's song "Breathe Me" blaring into my ears from my iPod nano, I burst into an explosion of sunshine onto Aldrich Avenue South. These days, I've been thinking a lot about the extraordinary last nine minutes of the TV show *Six Feet Under*'s finale, particularly because of the way Sia's song "Breathe Me" was incorporated perfectly, such that it was not just another musical coda. It was literally a coda to end all codas! (In the song, Sia had sung helplessly about feeling so small and beseeching help.)

As I pedaled south on Aldrich, I saw the apartment building where my sister Vivien once lived before she met her first wife. The windows of her garden-level apartment were blinded. I wondered about the squirrels that once came up to her windows. They were certainly in evidence, chasing each other up and down the tough trees lining the block. They, and full-grown rabbits bold enough to sit upright on lawns before bouncing away, are the main reason why my dog Rocky loves walking around this neighborhood. His ears come alive, his nose becomes wetter with anticipation, and his paws are poised to break free should I ever drop his leash. I thought about Rocky as I pushed my bike up West 22nd Street. I should strive to be alert and alive as he is whenever he is outside.

I turned left onto Bryant, swept at last of its winter gravel. With its parked cars gone for the day, it was as if the hard crystals of tears had finally caked and fell off my face. People on the sidewalk simply waved at me as I sped past. As I turned right again up on 24th Street for Colfax, I saw the artist John Largaespada's house where I met him for a ride to his preferred frame shop, where I chose the frame for his brilliant digital photograph homage "New York Movie," a vast improvement on Edward Hopper's painting of the same name, a month after I moved to Minneapolis.

Ahead of me were a block-long artillery of tree branches already filling out with the plumage of bud and bloom standing guard as I felt the blood of wanting to be alive again in my calves as I spun my pedals. Not just a mere "alive," but the never-afraid-of-life *alive*. Turning right on West 25th Street, I looked up at my old apartment on the third floor, which I'd loved so dearly and left for a man who eventually left me seven months later. A woman lives there in that apartment now, and her blinds looked a bit uneven. I thought of the slightly eccentric caretakers there, and how they'd turned very cold toward me once I left the building for the last time. It was almost as if I'd betrayed their faith and trust in me, as if I'd become flesh against blood.

I sailed west, past Emerson Avenue for Hennepin. As cars whizzed past, I waited for the lights to change and looked at the bus stop where I'd frequented for my buses downtown. Cars and trucks slowed down to a grudging stop. I zipped across Hennepin and headed over to the gas station where they offered free air. My tires had become flabby after sitting quietly in a dark garage. I pressed the tiny notch in the air pressure valve against the tiny tube of each tire and imagined hearing the hiss searing into my soul until I'm ready to burst.

I restarted my iPod and continued on West 25th. The houses became tonier as I flew down and turned left for the Lake of the

Isles. I looked both ways as I glided onto the bike trail. There was almost no one out even on this bright and sunny day, so I glanced at the expansive (and expensive) houses, which I'd memorized ever since I'd made the mistake of walking past the Euclid Street turnoff when I walked around the lake for the first time.

The tiny islands on my right had already starting to flesh out. I wondered what they were truly like, but as they were wildlife habitats, they were completely off-limits. They were the sort of places I loved exploring as a child back in Ironwood; their private nooks and crannies stoked the ashes of my imagination back to life and again. I recalled the priceless look of fear and exhilaration on my friend Paul's face when he and I dared to walk across the frozen surface of Lakes of the Isles one February.

Up and down the incline, I stood on my pedals to coast over the jaggy bumps under the greenway for Lake Bde Maka Ska. Once past the bridge, the path suddenly became an unbroken ribbon, repaved at last. I exulted in its smoothness by sitting fully in my saddle. The sun lathered its kisses all over my face.

I coasted into the wide, dark mouth of the bridge holding up West Lake Street, watching the narrow path and glancing behind whenever possible to ensure that there weren't any bike speed freaks zooming up from behind. Even on hot summer days, when I biked around those three lakes, I adored the bracing coolness whenever I went from Lake Bde Maka Ska to the Lake of the Isles.

Up and around, I reached for the start of Lake Bde Maka Ska's regular path; the lake has long been renowned for people watching and people walking to be watched. As I passed its boathouse, I ducked when I saw a hummingbird flounce seemingly at me but then turned away for blooms unknown. To say that I felt startled by the hummingbird was an understatement.

Dogs of all kinds and sizes, panting, bounced along with their owners, and I thought again of Rocky, how fortunate I was to have him in my life. One of the reasons why I'd loved dogs so much growing up was their unconditional love and acceptance of what I was at a time when no one wanted to be my friend. I was this deaf ugly duckling with ungainly hearing aids. Dogs never cared about any of that; they were simply there. They wagged in the *now*, and more so if I stroked their heads. I'll never forget how Rocky leaped onto my lap on the sofa, which I'd expressly forbidden, when I unexpectedly broke into tears and tried to apologize for letting him down during the chaos of moving out of my ex-boyfriend's apartment. He kept licking at my face until I had to stop crying and start laughing when he leaped off and returned with a stuffed squeaky toy that he wanted me to throw so he could fetch. The eagerness in his eyes made me remember that I had a life before the man who'd left me, and that I would do so after him. In fact, Rocky was *demanding* that I throw that dang toy across the long living room again! And again! And *again*. Dogs are so wonderful in the sense that they are a constant reminder of how life must go on, and a celebration of the seemingly mundane. Just ask their noses.

I slowed to a stop for a few gulps of water from my bottle. The walls of my insides, once parched, felt almost doubled in joy. As I inhaled the spritely lake air, I looked up at Lakewood Cemetery where I once sped on my 50 cc scooter before getting caught the summer before. I truly had no idea that scooters were not allowed in the cemetery, but then again, I suspect the dead never liked noise too much. Then I thought about how the cemetery had inspired a poem I'd written of love lost for the gardener-artist I'd fallen for a month after I moved into my new apartment, and how incredibly steadfast he had become as a friend. It had taken an unusually long time to compose each line; I had to prove to myself that in spite of my struggles with depression, I still had the chops to craft a strong and memorable poem.

As I started again, I vowed to keep moving without stopping. I pushed my pedals with gusto on the flat trail before turning left for the steep hill leading up to Lake Harriet. As I allowed the melodic thrusts of Sia's song to come over me, I reflected on how Claire Fisher, the *Six Feet Under* character who was driving away to the ebbs and flows of the song like I was, had to deal with the demons of doubt as an artist in the making. Was she self-centered? Of course. All artists are. How could they not be? It is their very perspective that enables them to stand out and remind everyone else that conformity is a curse. Artists are true warriors. They fight conventionality so that others don't have to.

I was surprised by how little effort it took me to conquer the hill, which was always the most difficult part of my three-lake ride. Perhaps I needed to feel solidarity with someone who truly understood what I had gone through, even with a fictional character filled with far more truth than some people I've met in my life, in order to feel inspired.

As I crossed the bridge, I caught sight of the empty trolley tracks. I reminded myself yet again that riding the trolley between the lakes was one of the things I must do, however seemingly trivial, if only to say that I'd done it. I did not want to die on a bed of regrets.

I propelled myself even faster toward Lake Harriet. As I turned left onto its bike path, I suddenly remembered meeting a straight couple late one cold January night on the same spot. They were walking a huge wheaten terrier. Rocky hadn't come into my life then, but the tenderness in their eyes was apparent when I took off my mitts and petted their dog. His jaw was caked with ice clumps of snow. I had been worried about how things would work out between Rocky and me, but they said not to worry. How so right they were! More and more people came out with their dogs; the afternoon sun had cranked up a few degrees.

Up ahead on my left was a bird sanctuary. I had to smile at the memory of stealing an incandescent kiss with a handsome date one early morning, and how comforting it was to embrace him, there, alone in the din of birds calling out to each other. It was a *déjà vu* moment from 1989 when I was dating a Republican lobbyist who'd moved from Washington, DC, to San Francisco. He took me up to the Muir Redwoods Forest. The giganticness and tallness and majesty of these trees took my breath away, and he nuzzled my neck as the mists dropped angelic sighs all around us. He thought he himself could take my breath away too, at least enough to convince me to relocate to San Francisco, but I eventually chose to stay put in New York.

I glanced at the infamous rose garden in the distance where, on one summer day, I took my DeafBlind friend John on a rented tandem bike around the three lakes. The roses were in full bloom then, and it was both touching and wonderful to see how my friend could detect by nose whether a rose was natural or a hybrid. I simply brought his hand to a new rose, and he'd bend down to sniff it. I'd look at the sign next to the bush, and he was always right which kind of rose it was. But right now, the roses were not out in full force yet, so I made a mental note to myself that I would bring Rocky there when the roses bloomed. It is always a joy to see his tail wag. Of the three lakes I biked, Lake Harriet—with its far more widespread tree shade—was always the coolest. As I coasted under the cocoon of buds ahead, I suddenly saw a flashback of my Texan friend James from behind, how simply he pedaled without moving much of his upper body, the week I didn't know I'd see him last. He was happy with all those trees surrounding him, as Dallas didn't have a whole lot of trees on the magnitude of Minnesota's.

I imagined him lying there in his expensive casket in the grave back in Dallas, and how I never got to give him a proper goodbye. Wasn't he supposed to stay around forever? All I kept thinking of was the last time I saw him: He stood still, his bearded jaw jutting out, rising up on the escalator at the Minneapolis-St. Paul Airport for his flight back to Texas. I didn't know it then, but if one wishes to believe that Heaven is above us, he was already headed for parts unknown.

Yes, I wanted to breathe him, as I had wanted to breathe in all that I loved. I kept pedaling, not dwelling how thirsty I was or how much I'd ached for all those people whom I knew and who had died. I'd shed enough tears, damn it! As I headed closer to the Lake Harriet Bandstand on my right, I saw a basset hound puppy roll over on her back and rub it against the grass, chortling all the while as her owner laughed at her antics. I thought of my previous dog Elsa, too, but then I chuckled at how Rocky had always done the exact same thing on the carpet in my apartment once I took off his neon orange vest that announced he was a hearing service dog. It was startling yet true how life does give you many gifts in such moments of clarity. It's a question of looking for them in the most unexpected places. Those make for the best gifts, because they remind you of the continuity between life and death. In that basset puppy, I saw both Elsa and Rocky chortling in the same moment; just as Elsa had died, so will Rocky, eventually. (I do not believe that it's a cosmic accident when in less than twenty-four hours of Elsa's death, I got an email describing Rocky to me for the first time.) I embrace the eventuality of his passing as much as I accept his feisty joy and energy into my own being. I accept that he will one day die as much as he will every day live. I must enjoy and love him now in all his moods. In order for me to be strong, I must also be weak. They are the two sides of the same coin. One cannot appreciate strength without weakness.

I pushed up the hill from the Lake Harriet Bandstand, which led to my favorite part of the ride around the lakes: the coasting from top to bottom back to Lake Bde Maka Ska. In that moment, I forgot all about everything that had come before but the sheer motion of my body flying through space and time down that steep hill. I thought nothing else but the wind of my bicycle carrying me forward to parts unknown, imaginary or not, beyond Lake Bde Maka Ska. The nagging questions of my life didn't matter so much anymore because I knew I would rediscover what it meant to be an artist, and that I would learn to trust my heart again. Breathing in all of life itself, I simply had to enjoy the questions more.

ACKNOWLEDGMENTS

The author wishes to thank the editors of these periodicals and anthologies in which the following pieces, a few of which were changed considerably, appeared:

Best Gay Romance 2015 (Felice Picano, ed.; Cleis Press): "Hands, Romancing" (formerly titled "Romancing of the Hands").

Clerc Scar: "Against a Universal Language," "*A Is for American*," and "Family Quotes."

Deaf Life: "'The Complexity of Real Life': An Interview with Nicolas Philibert" (formerly titled "'I Wanted to Show the Complexity of Real Life': Raymond Luczak's interview with Nicolas Philibert").

The Fire in Moonlight: Stories from the Radical Faeries 1971-2010 (Mark Thompson and Bo Young, eds.; White Crane Books): "Chants of Silence" (formerly subtitled "Notes of a Deaf Radical Faerie-in-Spirit").

Laurent: "*The General* (or, Why I Love Silent Films)" and "The Gogebic County Fair."

Marquette Monthly: "A Sort of Homecoming."

Poetry Magazine: "Forbidden Fruits in Our Hands."

RFD: "Missed Connections," "The Seeds of Truth," and "To Lose Is to Love."

SIGNews: "How I Became a Budding TV Star" and "On Steve Jobs."

Silent News: "In the Year 2122" (formerly titled "In the Year 2107").

We'll Never Have Paris: "Dreaming Differently" (formerly subtitled "Or, Why I Left New York").

Who's Yer Daddy?: Gay Writers Celebrate Their Mentors and Forerunners (Jim Elledge and David Groff, eds.; University of Wisconsin Press): "The World is Full of Orphans."

Wordgathering: "No More Savagery, Please: On *The Tribe*" (formerly subtitled "A Deaf Person's Review of *The Tribe*").

———

The pieces "Family Quotes" and "The Gogebic County Fair" were incorporated into "My Truest Home."

The piece "Learning to Breathe" first appeared on the author's personal blog.

The piece "My Friendship with Loneliness" was adapted from the author's keynote speech given at the Queer Disability Conference 2002 in Berkeley, California.

———

The author wishes to thank the following people who've helped with this book in ways both large and small: John Lee Clark, David Cummer (*in memoriam*), Kelly Davio, Lennard J. Davis, Adam Kauwenberg-Marsnik, Katie Lee, Angela Leppig, Robert McRuer, Deirdre Mullervy, Anthony Santos, and Tom Steele.

ABOUT THE AUTHOR

Raymond Luczak lost most of his hearing at the age of eight months due to double pneumonia and a high fever, but this was not detected until he was two-and-a-half years old. After all, he was just number seven in a hearing family of nine children growing up in Ironwood, a small mining town in Michigan's Upper Peninsula. Forbidden to sign, he was outfitted with a rechargeable hearing aid and started on speech therapy immediately. Because there were no programs for deaf children in Ironwood, he was brought two hours away to a speech therapy program in Houghton, where he would live with three foster families for a total of nine years.

Luczak is the author and editor of many books, including *Flannelwood: A Novel*, *QDA: A Queer Disability Anthology*, and *Compassion, Michigan: The Ironwood Stories*. His other titles include *From Heart into Art: Interviews with Deaf and Hard of Hearing Artists and Their Allies* and the award-winning Deaf gay novel *Men with Their Hands*. His book *once upon a twin: poems* was listed as a Top Ten U.P. Notable Book of the Year for 2021.

An inaugural Zoeglossia Fellow, he lives in Minneapolis, Minnesota.